ECONOMY
AND
ECOLOGY

Economy
and
Ecology

HOW CAPITALISM BROUGHT US TO THE BRINK

CHRISTOPHER ANDERSON

TATE PUBLISHING
AND ENTERPRISES, LLC

Published by Tate Publishing & Enterprises, LLC
127 E. Trade Center Terrace | Mustang, Oklahoma 73064 USA
1.888.361.9473 | www.tatepublishing.com

Tate Publishing is committed to excellence in the publishing industry. The company reflects the philosophy established by the founders, based on Psalm 68:11,
"The Lord gave the word and great was the company of those who published it."

Published in the United States of America

ISBN: 978-1-68333-267-1
1. Political Science / Political Economy
2. Business & Economics / Environmental Economics
16.04.25

This book is dedicated to the three most inspirational feminists in my life: Nancy Swanson, Emily Faulkner, and Corinne Anderson

ACKNOWLEDGEMENTS

I am indebted to Cherie Tucker of Grammarworks for her professional editing and advise on content, sharp technical eye, unsparing criticism and helpful suggestions.

CONTENTS

PREFACE

"The earth I tread on is not a dead, inert mass. It is a body, has a spirit, is organic, and fluid to the influence of its spirit, and to whatever particle of that spirit is in me." Henry David Thoreau

"Capitalism is inconsistent with democracy." Noam Chomsky

According to the Japan Meteorological Society, March through July were the hottest months since they began keeping records back in 1880. 2014 was the hottest year on record, and 2015 is predicted to be even hotter.

Forest fires are raging out of control throughout the drought-stricken country. A record-breaking heat wave in India killed hundreds of people. Central Europe is cooking in unseasonably intense heat, over 32 degrees Celsius, an incredible 12 degrees hotter than usual. In Japan, 1,037 people were hospitalized because of the heat.

The Pentagon has warned that summers in the future are going to bring increased suffering, food loss, disease, with decreasing quality of air and water, mass migrations, and an increased security risk for the U.S.

The famous Joshua trees in the Joshua Tree National Park are dying.

White beetle infestation is killing trees in the northern United States and Canada. Polar bears in the Arctic and penguins in Antarctica are starving.

As Australia continues to suffer from devastating droughts, Prime Minister Tony Abbot has succeeded in a campaign pledge to eliminate the carbon tax, leaving the nation with no legislated policy to limit carbon emissions, calling the tax "useless and destructive." He is attempting to build support for a coalition to derail international efforts to battle climate change. Australian born entrepreneur Robert Murdoch has said that man-made climate change should be looked at with great skepticism.

A recent report from Mission Ocean declared that "the ocean is in decline, habitat destruction, biodiversity loss, overfishing, pollution, climate change and ocean acidification are pushing the ocean system to the point of collapse."

The Pacific island of Kiribati—home to 100,000 people—is shrinking as rising sea levels swallow up the land. They are preparing to evacuate the people to the second largest island in the Fijis.

Families living on the coast of Isle de Jean Charles in Louisiana are being forced to flee their multi-generational homes due to rising sea levels.

According to ecologists and land planners in Oakland, California, neighborhoods on the coast are likely to be forced back by rising seas and increasing storms. Snowpack in California that historically supplies one-third the water to the state is melting in summer swelter, and

Governor Jerry Brown has declared a state emergency, limiting water use (except on agri-businesses, of course).

Record level "100-year floods" are now a regular occurrence in the Midwest. Tornadoes are happening on a daily basis in the spring and summer.

In Alaska recorded one-quarter of its usual annual rainfall in a single 24-hour day.

Virginia Democrats and Republicans are putting partisan politics aside as they try to figure out what to do about their coast being gobbled up by the sea.

Greenland's ice sheet is melting. According to National Geoscience, if the entire ice sheet melts, the ocean will rise by 24 feet.

And yet, the Republican majority in this country has not accepted man-made climate change as real. At least most of them now have finally acceded that climate change exists. And while most Democrats are in unison of the reality of climate change, their rhetoric is unfortunately not in sync with their actions.

The BBC, however, unlike the major networks in the U.S. is facing reality, refusing to give any more airtime to climate change deniers.

U.S. Interior Secretary Sally Jewell recently reported that she is witnessing the effects of climate change in every national park she visits. That didn't keep her and the Obama administration from allowing Shell Oil to search for oil in the melting Arctic.

An international group of scientists recently concluded that existing extinction rates are 1,000 times higher than normal and that the Earth is on the brink of a man-made extinction catastrophe equal to the extinction of the dinosaurs 65 million years ago.

Amidst all this, the world economy is in chaos, and the social structure in virtually every country in the world is collapsing and rebelling.

Since the title of this book is "Economy and Ecology" you might wonder what the ecology has to do with the economy. Unfortunately, a lot. As I shall point out in the following chapters, it is the world economy, specifically a world *capitalist* economy that despite its modest regulations and restrictions over corporate power these last two centuries has caused the Earth to be on the brink of ecological catastrophe. And the philanthropic billionaires are not going to save us, despite their narcissistic beliefs to the contrary. The reason they are not going to save us is because their "solutions" lie in the very economic system that brought us here: capitalism.

October 2015

PART I

FREE MARKET CAPITALISM

CHAPTER 1

The United States Empire currently leads the world economy. And like the last days of Rome, that empire is on the verge of extinction, and with it they are taking most of the species that exist on the planet, including the human species.

Historically, most empires last about 200 years. Ours began in 1776. We are now in what historians called the last days of Rome: the Age of Decadence.

The debasement of the currency, representative in the economic collapse of 2008, is symptomatic of this declining empire. We are kept distracted with a superficially bloated stock market, meaningless entertainment like "Dancing With the Stars", sports, celebratory worship, advertising, reality TV, and amateur song and dance routines—but it will not stop the inevitable collapse.

The Baby Boomers were brought up in this beginning age of decadence, and in the sixties, they rebelled. Novels such as *The Catcher in the Rye*, *Catch-22*, *On the Road*, and films such as *Rebel Without a*

Cause, Hud, and *Easy Rider*—were symbolic to this rising rebellion. They ended a meaningless war, protested pollution and nuclear power, demanded civil and individual rights, and touted back to the land sentiments, sexual freedom, and an end to an oppressive economic system.

And the corporatists fought back. They formed institutions such as the Heritage Foundation, the Cato Institute, and the Ayn Rand Institute. The climate change denial movement began here. Even the social gains won by the New Deal and Keynesian economics were under attack. This counterrevolution really came of age during the Reagan Administration, which preached that corporate greed is good because it will "trickle down" on the rest of us and make us all wealthy. This philosophy is still being preached successfully by the right, even infecting former "liberals" in the Democratic Party, maintaining that the only reason it hasn't trickled down to the masses (in fact has become worse) is due to obstacles presented by the Left. But there is no genuine Left with any power in this country anymore. It has been replaced by a corporate led plutocracy.

Subsidies for the oil, coal, and gas companies continue unabated. Factories continue to be allowed to pollute. Car manufacturers continue to make vehicles that emit CO_2, the nuclear industry is allowed to carry on despite Fukushima, the most catastrophic meltdown in history, even worse than Chernobyl, renewable alternatives continue to be repressed—all because our politicians continue to kowtow to corporations who cannot think past their next quarterly report.

It is not just right wing fanatics who see climate change as an affront to their most cherished values, it is also the pseudo left represented in the Democratic Party. To end unbridled free enterprise is unthinkable.

In 2007 a Harris poll showed that 71% of Americans believed that climate change was caused by the release of CO_2 into the atmosphere. By 2009, the figure dropped to 51%, and by 2011 more than half of Americans didn't believe it. What happened? As we keep experiencing more droughts, floods, fires, and extreme storms—more people than ever disbelieve what 97% of the climate scientists say is real.

What happened is an intense conditioning by the corporate led major media to deny its existence. They brought "debate" into a condition that is no longer debatable, scientists verses right wing capitalists who want to maintain business as usual despite the obvious.

This conditioning began in the 70s as the baby boomers began to sell out and become ardent capitalists, which was not entirely their fault (see my book *What Happened to the Love Generation? How the Boomers Blew It*). There was a powerful establishment that contributed to this; however, there are few boomers today who are seriously tackling the critical issue of climate change; they are leaving it to their children and grandchildren, at a time when it has likely passed the tipping point. We've known about climate change for thirty years. We should have been doing something about it then, but we didn't. There are a lot of comfortable liberals in the boomer generation today. They are changing light bulbs with LEDs, purchasing hybrid vehicles, buying organic (mainly for their personal health), and sitting back patting themselves on the back. But guess what—it isn't nearly enough. You blew it, boomers (and I admit to being one of them), and now the species on earth are going extinct at a rate of 200 a day.

The marketing of processed food has resulted in a society of obese like the last days of Rome, while the rest of the world is suffering famines, droughts, catastrophic storms, floods, social unrest, and rebellion.

It's almost Biblical.

Banks create money out of nothing, and then loan it to us with interest. This money is called "fiat" money, and the system is designed so that it all ends up back in the hands of the wealthy.

Milton Friedman, who taught at the Chicago School of Economics, pushed a system of laissez-faire economics. "Laissez-faire economics", is a non-interventionist form of capitalism—allowing the market to regulate itself without government interference. It rejects Keynesian economics, which had been used by FDR to get us out of the Great Depression, reigning in corporate greed and irresponsibility. Friedman promoted what he called "monetarism". Ayn Rand in her two philosophical novels *The Fountainhead* and *Atlas Shrugged* promoted this belief system. Alan Greenspan was a personal friend of Rand's, and he became the Federal Reserve Chairman from 1987 to 2008, from Reagan to Obama, pushing this neoliberal agenda. Ronald Reagan in the U.S. and Margaret Thatcher in Great Britain, instituted this neoliberal model during their times in office, and since then every President in the United States and every Prime Minister in Great Britain has more or less carried on with this economic model, bringing the world to where it is today, on the verge of economic and ecological collapse.

When Bill Clinton became president he signed a bill that ended Glass-Steagall, which had been instituted by FDR to ensure that investors could speculate only with their own money, and not the savings of Americans. After Clinton ended Glass-Steagall, the speculators were allowed to gamble recklessly with the money sitting in Americans' savings accounts. This led to the financial crisis of 2008, when everyone's savings, 401Ks and IRAs were on the verge of being zero. The federal government had to loan over a trillion dollars to the large banks. Not one person went to jail for this unscrupulous financial speculation, except for Bernie Madoff, who was used as a scapegoat for doing exactly what the large banks were doing.

The stock market rebounded, and currently, they are doing it all over again, because the Congress and the President refuse to reinstate Glass-Steagall, or any regulatory principle like it. Thus we have a system of socialism for the "too big to fail" banks, and capitalism for the rest of us. Another global pyramid scam is now in the making.

Despite what our leaders are constantly telling us, we do not have a democracy in this country, we have a plutocracy: a government for and by the rich. We never have had a democracy. Our forefathers formed a "republic" in which only rich, Caucasian landowners could vote in legislatures, which represent their interests. Although civil rights legislation slowly increased representation, we still have a society that through massive lobbying and campaign contributions by the rich to our politicians best represents the interests of the rich; and corporations such as Goldman-Sachs are allowed to speculate as much money as they want, and when they lose it, the American taxpayer is there to bail them out.

Milton Friedman's neo-classical capitalist model promoted the idea that by giving all the money to the rich it would "trickle down" on the rest of us, with jobs, income, etc. The only problem with this logical philosophy is that the rich didn't do it. They didn't put money into the economy with industry, et cetera.; they speculated with it, put it in overseas bank accounts, and avoided paying taxes. They paid themselves top salaries, bonuses and stock options for essentially doing nothing productive.

And then they pushed this agenda onto the rest of the world, loaning money to "Third World" countries so that corporations could extract the resources of that country (polluting the environment), and exploit the workers (paying them slave wages), so they could make even more money.

To add insult to injury, chemical corporations such as Monsanto introduced genetically modified seeds to the world environment, ruining and polluting the land, compromising health and devastating farmers, who could no longer use the seeds from the plants. The result has been environmental catastrophe and worldwide social unrest, causing billions of people to revolt. That's pretty much it in a nutshell, folks. The end.

So when the farmers can no longer farm their ruined land and the fishermen can no longer fish from overfished and polluted oceans, they naturally rebel, join extremist groups, and we call them "terrorists."

In the U.S., 9/11 has been presented to us as one of the most devilish examples of terrorism ever. But there is another 9/11, one we Americans seldom hear about, and that is the terrorism committed on 9/11/1973, when in Chile, the democratically elected Marxist president Salvador Allende was murdered by a CIA inspired coup d'état, who then put into power the fascist dictator Augusto Pinochet, resulting in 17 years of terrorism, murder, and torture. This takeover and subsequent dictatorship was lauded by none other than Milton Friedman and his model of neoliberalism capitalism, and supported by American Presidents from Nixon to Clinton. Under the influence of this free market-oriented neoliberal "Chicago Boys" influence, the military government implemented economic reforms, including stabilizing currency, cutting tariffs, opening Chile's markets to global trade, restricting labor unions, privatizing social security, and privatizing all state-controlled industries, all the while murdering over 3,000 people and imprisoning and torturing 30,000. The Chileans finally managed to oust Pinochet in 1990, who fled and was about to be extradited and tried for terrorism when he died in 2006.

CHAPTER 2

In Germany after World War II the German government cancelled all German debt, other than what employers owed employees. The people actually owned their homes free and clear. They rebuilt their economy from ground zero.

The allies also forgave their debts as well as those of Japan, and The Marshall Plan gave them money to rebuild. Germany has now become probably the most successful economic country in the world, with a huge surplus, even while paying their workers decent pay and benefits, including free education through college, and a fully funded infrastructure, including a high-speed rail system. They also have a huge trade surplus, which indicates that the reasons we Americans were given for offshoring jobs in the United States because of our high wages and benefits is nonsense. German automakers make about $60 an hour and still manage to sell their cars.

In 2008, the United States was enthralled with a young charismatic senator by the name of Barack Obama. It was obvious by his rhetoric to the more sensible of us that he was just another pawn for the corporate elite, but we elected him anyway for the usual lesser of two evils reason.

When the economy crashed, rather than do what Germany did after World War II (with the help of the Marshall Plan) and FDR did during the Great Depression, which is to forgive the mortgages of strapped mortgage holders, George W. Bush and then Obama bailed out the large banks, who in turn foreclosed on these mortgage holders and flipped the homes to make even more money.

Both Roosevelts, Theodore and his distant cousin Franklin, took on the big banks. Teddy also created a national parks system that rebuilt the country's forests, preventing most of our country from being clear-cut, which had already happened in places such as Ireland and New Zealand. Naturalist John Muir even convinced Teddy that it was immoral to hunt recreationally. Ever since JFK was assassinated (more on that later), a neoliberal economic principle has ruined the earth through extraction of resources. Since Teddy Roosevelt's time, 95% of all life forms on earth have gone extinct. We are quickly losing that which we humans need to survive. We are going through an unprecedented mass extinction for one reason and one reason only: the obsession for private profits.

Obama entered office in 2008 talking about healing the planet and continued to talk about it with his as usual brilliant rhetoric, but in his six years in office his actions to do something about global warming have been pretty much zilch.

When salmon swim upstream to spawn and die, species such as bears and large cats eat the fish and then their scat fertilizes the forests with nitrogen and other minerals. No salmon: no healthy forests. This is just one example of what took billions of years for nature to evolve to a near perfect synchronization with nature, and about 300 years for humans to destroy it. This monetary means of exchange, resulting in pollution of land, air and water; transfer of invasive species; removal of forests; and a nuanced conspiracy of overpopulation for means of exploitation, all have interfered with the miracle of nature. You can call it the grace of God or you can call it natural science. You can look at it from an aesthetic viewpoint, such as how sad it will be not to have such beautiful animals such as lions and tigers, or we can look at it selfishly, realizing that we humans cannot survive without the other species on which we depend for survival.

The CO_2 we have dumped into the air and water not so much for energy as for private profits has probably put the climate past the tipping point.

Humans consume 50% of the food on earth, and its increase in population has become unsustainable, its system of capitalism taking and taking and not giving back. One-half of the population uses two-thirds of the resources. In the United States we have a luxury economy, and the rest of the world has been trying to catch up, especially China, parts of which now have the most polluted air on earth, mostly from burning coal.

We have taken Darwin's theory on survival and created a monetary system that has turned into an obsession to have more than what we need to subsist. Once human needs were satisfied, it was not enough. Studies on million dollar lottery winners have shown that most of them eventually go bankrupt. They have millions and it's not enough to sustain them; they become obsessed with accumulating more stuff than their millions can afford: RV's, bigger homes, the most expensive vehicles, and so on, until they are head over heels in debt and in bankruptcy court.

I'm sure most people sincerely care about the environment and the environment that they are leaving for their descendants. I'm sure Obama worries about the future world his two daughters will inherit. But it doesn't seem to stop people from indulging in the very processes that contribute to our eventual demise. We indulge in that which gives us immediate satisfaction.

We abide in what is called Nature Deficit Disorder, which is having no real consciousness of what we feel are our basic needs: food, transportation, warm houses in the winter and cool houses in the hot summer, smart phones, TVs, refrigeration. Every part of our day has at its roots the destruction of the environment.

According to recent studies, at least 200 species are going extinct every day. Ninety percent of the large fish in the ocean are gone. The largest animal species that exists is the whale, an extremely complex mammal that is stunningly intelligent, beautiful, with intense emotional feelings for family. We have spent hundreds of years hunting this incredibly marvelous animal to near extinction. Even today, there are three countries that haven't stopped killing whales despite trifling efforts to stop them: Russia, Japan and Norway.

Is there anything more beautiful than a Bengali Tiger, a polar bear or a redwood tree? This beauty exists in nature due to billions of years of adapting positively to the environment, and humanity's actions in just the blink of an eye have brought this beauty to the edge of extinction.

CHAPTER 3

The modern day dismantling of the middle class began with Ronald Reagan. Before Reagan was elected, large employers such as Boeing, Weyerhaeuser, GM, etc. provided decent wages and benefits. Today we have companies such as Walmart, Starbucks and Amazon in the vanguard of employment, paying most of their workers as little as they can get away with, and thanks to Reagan and his supply-side economic principles, most of these workers barely make enough money to get by alongside a huge army of unemployed and homeless.

Today companies that had once paid their workers well are taking advantage of this economic principle as well. Boeing has succeeded in ending the guaranteed pension plans and making the workers pay more for their health care.

Those who are lucky to have jobs at all now fret over their 401Ks rather than look forward to a guaranteed retirement pension.

And our tax system is designed to ensure that income generated flows through the corporation and the owners of capital without being seriously siphoned off by the state and the tax system for other purposes.

A French economist, Thomas Picketty, recently got a lot of press with his book, *Capital in the 21st Century*. Paul Krugman and others in the liberal news media gave this book a lot of positive hype. The book specifically discusses the accelerating of capital income and the concentration of wealth on the owner class. Picketty mentions that the wealthiest have been increasing their wealth steadily during good times and bad and that the recessions that have occurred in the U.S. since 1980, including the major one in 2008, have not had a negative effect on the top 1%, while working families have barely maintained their incomes and standards of living even during the best of times, and working class households are stagnating or declining in terms of real wages. In short, the rich have gotten richer and the poor have gotten poorer—hardly news for most of us. Reducing labor costs is one major way income has increased for the wealthiest 1%, as well as income generated from financial speculation, capital gains, dividends, interest, real estate and rent. Governments through lobbying and business threats to leave town, leave the onus of taxation increasingly on the working class, reducing corporate income taxes. The owners of capital manipulate the financial system for private gain and exploitation of labor.

Another economic philosopher wrote about this exact phenomenon 150 years ago. His name was Karl Marx.

Picketty and others of liberal economic thought such as Paul Krugman and Robert Reich continue to cover this superficially while failing to offer definitive solutions, basically still pushing capitalism. Right or wrong, Marx did, at least until he was writing *Capital*, left unfinished when he died.

Part of government's job in keeping us uninformed is to maintain false statistics. For example, as soon as the unemployed exhaust their unemployment compensation, they stop being a statistic. They also count part-time work as being employed. The trend in income disparity is consequently worse than reported.

Also unreported is the current means of transferring money that had once been put into pension trusts now being put into 401Ks, which are also designed to return to the owners of capital during stock market crashes. There are also continued cutbacks in benefits, especially healthcare, the later of which employees are increasingly forced to pay more into out of their paychecks. Wages are further paid to the rich through credit and debt, the interest on which of course goes to corporations, and the rich.

Another category that needs calculating is the increasing burden on the working class to pay into social security and Medicare, benefits of which are increasingly reduced in a lame excuse of "austerity." The bad press the Veterans Administration and IRS receives is symbolic of this, as government programs are stretched thin due to decreasing monies and the mainstream press is conveniently there to put the blame on the program itself, subliminally giving us the message: "See? Socialism doesn't work." John McCain has suggested that the government give money to veterans to go to private hospitals, a blatant form of privatization. This same privatization scheme is being formed on Social Security and Medicare. Obamacare is symbolic of this trend as our taxes go for individuals to use on private health care.

And then stagnant wages are further reduced through inflation, in which adjustments for real wages are not identified. Seattle is getting a lot of liberal hype for implementing a $15 an hour plan which is currently actually a $11 an hour plan not to be fully implemented to $15 an hour until 2025, which will by then be eaten away by inflation.

And we are programmed to idolize billionaires such as Steve Jobs and Bill Gates. And it's probably true that these two talented guys were/are nice enough guys as far it goes. They also were/are undoubtedly woefully ignorant and in denial of their own impact on the economy and the environment. Bill Gates probably really believes his merger with Monsanto to provide genetically modified foods will solve the hunger problem of the world.

Or perhaps not. I have another theory. Aware of the problem of overpopulation, Gates has introduced GMOs to induce mass starvation, because that is going to be the result. GMOs don't work. They ruin farmland, kill livestock, and poison people. They have been thrust upon the consumer without proper testing and now are ruining our health. How he could not know this confounds me, since the evidence is incontrovertible and thus my theory of reducing the world of billions of inhabitants. Might be a good plan after all. Whales good; people bad. This is said with tongue only partly in cheek.

Naomi Klein wrote a brilliant book called *The Shock Doctrine* about the consequences of the neo-classical, or neoliberal, principle, writing about many infamous human rights violations due to the policies of dictators such as Pinochet in Chile. According to Klein, neoliberalism posits that when a country develops a strong middle class, it needs a major crisis, or "shock" to put society back in its place, scrounging desperately for a piece of the pie. Eliminating social programs such as government pensions, education, socialized medicine and so forth and implementing total privatization does this. It was done in Chile, in Argentina, and it was done after Hurricane Katrina, according to Klein. Natural disasters are convenient for shock doctrinaires as well.

As a valid economic theory this of course works—for the rich. It creates a minority of rich and a majority of poor. Marx said that the result of this inequality would produce a revolution, preferably peacefully, violently if necessary, but an inevitable one nevertheless, and eventual democratic socialism.

Today, Ayn Rand's objectivist philosophy continues to be popular with young people. Rand and writer Alexander Solzhenitsyn were two Russians of the same generation who witnessed the horrors of Stalin, and associated these horrors with Marxism. They both believed that the only answer to Stalin, and as such, Marxism, was laissez-faire capitalism. The neoliberal economy persisted, won out, and here we are, the world on the brink of catastrophe. Is it that simple? Well yes, I believe it is. It's what this book is about.

Alternative technologies exist today to replace the extraction of natural resources for energy. But the interests of coal, oil, agribusiness (wheat corn, soy, cattle, etc.) nuclear and natural gas still hold power in Washington D.C. with their campaign contributions and lobbying.

These industries are subsidized, given government money to ruin the earth and receive huge profits from it. Nuclear power, which is so expensive to operate that it would be impossible to function without government subsidies, is the most blatant insult to laissez-faire capitalism that exists. Even after what happened at Fukushima, with nuclear waste still leaking into the ocean as of this writing, Obama still refers to as a "green" source.

The administration still continues to enable the current conditions. The decision on whether or not to build the Keystone XL pipeline is still on hold, when there is only one decision to make: don't build it. But right now land through the Midwest is being dug up in anticipation of it being built.

When there are rowdy disruptions on the capitalist system, such as the Occupy Movement, the establishment responds with its military power and quickly shuts it down. The Democrats make "green friendly" statements without actually doing anything of real consequence to fix things. The banksters are bailed out while the poor continue to suffer as their homes are repossessed.

I tie in economy with ecology because they co-exist as entities that are expected by us, the "people" to push for our well-being and survival. Our constitutional right for the "pursuit of happiness" includes a happy and healthy planet with sustainable species.

To counter the damage done by global warming, it is necessary for the legislatures we elect to be in charge of what needs to be done. The nations forefathers created a republic supposedly to represent our interests and in turn the interests of the earth, which after all is in our interests as well.

Next to China, the U.S. puts more CO_2 into the atmosphere than any other country on earth, and it was the U.S. and China that were the only two countries who refused to sign onto mandatory cutbacks in CO_2 emissions at the Copenhagen environmental summit.

Environmental activism such as Bill McKibben's 350. org operates under the auspices of capitalism. McKibben campaigned for Obama, then criticized him for not doing enough for the environment, and then in 2012, campaigned for him *again*. Liberal radio pundits such as Thom Hartmann do the same. Liberal pundits such as Stephanie Miller and Rachel Madow are incapable of making any criticism of Obama at all. McKibben's 350. org is financed by the Rockefeller family, one of the most exploitive families of all time. This operation is staffed by people who receive six-figure incomes. For these people global warming is a source of employment.

Earth Day was launched in 1970 in response to what we were then calling "the Greenhouse effect". That was 44 years ago. And every April we get into our Toyota Priuses and drive somewhere to plant a seedling.

We all want to save the earth, but it won't happen until we get to the root cause of the malaise, and it isn't just Fox News and Republicans who refuse to do something about global warming. It is also the pseudo-liberals in the Democratic Party, who keep being subsidized by the engines of climate change.

One of the biggest misconceptions about rescuing the environment is that it can be done with the very economic system that caused the crisis in the first place: free enterprise. Billionaires such as Bill Gates, Michael Bloomberg, Warren Buffett, Richard Branson, Dick Knight, and many others are so delusional in their narcissism that they think their superior brains can come up with such a technology to save us. The implication here is that we can continue our wasteful and polluting ways because they will magically come up with a technology to counter it.

Warren Buffet is one who talks routinely about arresting climate change, while at the same time owns several coal-burning companies and holds interest in ExxonMobil and the tar sands-extracting company Suncor. Like Obama, he talks about "clean coal", an oxymoron if there ever was one. Michael Bloomberg has given huge sums of money to the Sierra Club and the Environmental Defense Fund while at the same time he has helped set up a firm specializing in oil and gas assets. Such is the contradiction in capitalism and environmentalism: like mixing oil and water.

Bill Gates talks much about climate change concerns while investing heavily in BP, ExxonMobil, and Monsanto, the latter of which is in the process of ruining the globe's food supply with GMOs and the pesticides that go with it. Gates is a major investor in nuclear power, another major contributor the climate change, as well as the continuing inevitable disasters such as the nuclear meltdowns at Chernobyl and Fukushima, the consequences of which we are still suffering. (Don't eat Pacific salmon; the last I heard the Fukushima plant is still leaking nuclear waste into the Pacific Ocean).

Gates has invested heavily in pursuing a technology to block the sun, such as shooting volcanic sulfur into the air. The obvious side effect of this—like all reckless pursuits of free enterprise—is the unpredictable consequences when we try to manipulate the Laws of Nature.

Dick Knight talks about "an initiative to develop technology to recycle CO_2 directly into the air." Such ideas suggest not polluting just once, but recycling it over and over—for profit, of course.

It is beyond the comprehension of these narcissistic sociopaths to even consider the horrid possibility that they would have to give up their precious free enterprise system and reduce growth, not contribute to it in a never-ending cycle of ravaging the Earth's resources in a finite world.

The climate scientists tell us that the only way to counter climate change is to keep the fossil fuels in the ground. As we now know, fossil fuels are the result of eons of living things dying and decomposing. It is literally is (or was) a humongous underground compost pile. It absorbs CO_2 and keeps the Earth stable. It is part of the Earth's complicated and evolving ecosystem.

Chapter 4

Alexander Hamilton proposed putting what he called "tariffs" on imports to protect manufacturing in the U.S. He also proposed giving American industries subsidies in order to be globally competitive. The Wagner Act of 1935 guaranteed Americans the right to form labor unions and bargain collectively. By the 1900s, the U.S. had emerged as a powerful economic force. By the 1950s there was a $15 billion trade surplus, and the U.S. was the most powerful manufacturing force in the world.

In 1890, the signing of the Sherman Antitrust Act by Teddy Roosevelt prevented companies from getting too big, his target specifically John D. Rockefeller, who had monopolized the oil and gas industries and become the richest person on the planet. Rockefeller was famous for dolling out ten cents for tips in restaurants.

Standard Oil was divided into 33 separate companies. It was illegal for a company to operate against public interest. FDR created the Securities Exchange Commission (SEC), which was designed to regulate the stock market and the

Federal Deposit Insurance Corporation (FDIC) which insured the people's bank deposits, and the Glass-Steagall Act, which mandated that banks couldn't speculate with the people's deposits. With these reforms, Wall Street was held in check, and FDR was extremely popular as a result of these reforms and other government programs that put people back to work during the Great Depression.

For the next 60 years, the stock market was held in check and went without a major crash, resulting in the most stable economic period in history.

In 1959, Fidel Castro marched into Havana with a rag-tag troupe of revolutionaries and ousted the Batista dictatorship. The United States had nebulously supported Castro, feeling Batista was a nuisance, and expecting Castro to create a capitalist democracy. Castro wore a cross around his neck to give the impression he was a staunch Catholic. As soon as he was in power, however, he stunned Washington D.C. by kicking out all the American corporations and the Mafioso, the later of which controlled the casinos.

Eisenhower and the C.I.A. decided that Castro had to go, and they concocted a plan to oust him. They would use Cuban expatriates to attack Havana, and when this inevitably failed they would bomb the country and send in the marines. Richard Nixon as vice-president was well aware of this plan, and planned to implement it as soon as he was elected president.

Nixon was defeated and they had to present this plan to a young and brilliant, but woefully naive John F. Kennedy. Kennedy was a staunch anti-communist as much as the next rich guy, but balked at the world criticism that would result if he followed the nationals in with American air power and a marine invasion. He allowed the Bay of Pigs invasion to proceed—without backing it up with an American invasion.

The nationals were quickly killed or arrested by Castro's military, and the C.I.A. was enraged. So was Kennedy, who refused to go along with further anti-Castro plans.

He also saw that Vietnam was looking like a hopeless, pointless quagmire, and huddled with his brother Robert and his Defense Secretary Robert McNamara with a plan to withdraw.

The Kennedys also were quite aware that the mafia in the country was out of control. J. Edgar Hoover as long-time head of the F.B.I. was more obsessed with stopping the spread of communism than in ending organized crime. JFK put his Attorney-General brother in charge of a committee to reign in organized crime. Hoover was enraged.

In talks with his Joint Chiefs of Staff, Kennedy was told that it was necessary to launch a nuclear war to contain communism. Kennedy was stunned to realize his Joint Chiefs were a crew of right wing lunatics and was in a quandary what to do about it.

Then, told that the Soviet Union had installed nuclear weapons in Cuba aimed at the United States, his military advisors told him he had no choice but to invade Cuba. Soviet warships were coming from the Soviet Union to the Gulf of Mexico and the world teetered on a impending nuclear war. Frantically, and with brilliant self-control, Kennedy engaged in a series of negotiations with Premier Nikita S. Khrushchev, agreeing to remove nuclear weapons in Turkey aimed at the Soviet Union if Khrushchev would remove his missiles in Cuba. Khrushchev agreed, and an almost certain nuclear holocaust was avoided by the skin of its teeth.

But this only served to enrage Kennedy's cabinet members even more. The C.I.A., the F.B.I. and even the Secret Service despised Kennedy. The Mafia was enraged that they had lost their casinos in Cuba. The C.I.A. and the mafia were in cahoots and came up with a plan to murder Kennedy, using a C.I.A. underling called Lee Harvey Oswald as a patsy to assassinate Kennedy, first attempted in Chicago, and when that was thwarted, again attempted in Dallas, which was successful.

Jack Ruby, associated with the Mafia and on orders from the C.I.A. assassinated Oswald to keep him from talking, and and while he was awaiting trial, conveniently died of cancer.

The Warren Commission appointed to investigate the assassination ignored people who had witnessed armed Secret Service men firing shots on the famous "grassy knoll" and the report was whitewashed, concluding that the lunatic, Lee Harvey Oswald, acted alone.

The assassination of John F. Kennedy spun the world on its axis.

Everything that has occurred since has culminated in the world we inhabit today, one on the brink of ecological and/or nuclear devastation, and ruled by transnational mega-corporations, with never-ending military conflicts throughout the Middle East, plundering and killing in a modern day colonial expansion and private profits for military corporations. Since Kennedy, Democrat and Republican alike have groveled to what Eisenhower tried to subliminally warn us about in his resignation speech in 1960 about the dangers of the "military industrial complex". Today U.S. military operations dominate the world, with over 10,000 military bases. Nearly half of our federal taxes go to the military.

We have ongoing military operations in Iraq, Yemen, Afghanistan, Pakistan, and throughout the Mideast. Who benefits from this huge military presence? Certainly not the countries who continue to be transgressed, or the people of these countries held in check and kept poor and impoverished; or the the soldiers we send who are killed, wounded, and come home with PTSD to a Veterans Administration that keeps getting funding cuts. Who benefits are the military contractors such as Boeing, General Dynamics, Lockheed/Martin, etc., as well as the mercenary corporations such as Blackwater, or XE Services or whatever they call themselves these days. Our military bases throughout the world are keeping the world safe for corporate power.

Thanks to brave whistleblowers such as Chelsea Manning, Julian Assange, Edward Snowden, and other brave journalistic sources mainly through a free internet (for now), we are kept aware of U.S. abuses, its torture, drone strikes that have murdered innocent people, and the unconstitutional surveillance by our government a la ever prescient Orwell's *1984*.

CHAPTER 5

In the 50s and 60s there was a lot of futuristic discourse about technology creating a 21st Century with more time for leisure and creativity. This future could have been a reality if not for one profound roadblock: capitalism. Capitalism is not designed for the benefit of the masses; it is designed for the ruling class. In fact, it is considered not beneficial by the ruling class that the masses have too much time on their hands to think creatively. This was realized in the 60s when the generation that FDR created with a strong middle class was able to send their kids to college, and in giving the youth opportunity to think creatively, these kids rebelled against the status quo. The establishment responded and shut the Movement down.

So what happened is that these advancements in technology created a minority of billionaires while the rest of the population was working sixty hours a week or else unemployed, with lives more stressed and complicated than ever. The computer age has not made our lives easier, in fact quite the opposite.

Moammar al-Gadhafi was the son of an impoverished Bedouin goat herder. He became a revolutionary. He took power in Libya in a 1969 coup d'état. He discarded the monarchy and declared Libya a republic, producing what he called "Islamic socialism". He nationalized the oil industry, bolstered the military, and introduced social programs.

He was also a megalomaniac who had lived his life as a warrior. As a result, he suffered from PTSD and paranoia. But since the country was awash in oil, he had an idea that he thought would be beneficial to his people and make him extremely popular: Nobody was required to work. Everyone was provided an income. All labor was imported. The oil proceeds stayed in the country from which it was produced.

While this obviously was extremely popular with the people of Libya, he was despised by the transnational oil companies, and their lackeys, the power structure in Washington D.C. and London. A propaganda campaign was put into place to demonize him. Reagan bombed his tent, killing one of his children. Gadhafi grieved and then capitulated to the global power structure. The people of Libya began to suffer and they rebelled. A civil war broke out, the revolution backed by NATO. Gaddafi was sodomized with a sword. This is just one example of what is happening throughout the Mideast.

But I digress. President Reagan cut the tax rate of the rich from 70% to 28%, a 70% tax rate that had been in place since FDR and had contributed to a strong middle class while still allowing the rich to live extremely well.

Today, despite production increases of 400%, the middle class for the most part has been decimated, wages have fallen when compared to inflation, benefits have decreased, and college kids are saddled with huge debts.

There is no reason we could not have had this leisure/ creative society, with short workweeks and a comfortable living standard. The greed inherent in the economic philosophy of Hayek and Friedman's free enterprise prevents it. This greed is so entrenched and psychotic in the mindset of our leaders that they don't even care that most of the world's species are on the precipice of extinction, and of course with it their precious capitalist economy, similar to the rich capitalists in FDR's time who couldn't see that FDR was saving their ass's.

Probably the most blatant example of this psychopathic mindset is Walmart and the Walton family who are nothing like the patrician who started the business, Sam Walton. The six Waltons are collectively the richest family on earth, and they maintain this wealth with the exploitation of their workers and slave wages overseas. The average "associate" at Wal-Mart makes $27,000 a year. This is a crime. It is legal, but it is a crime nevertheless.

In his Inaugural Address in 1981 Ronald Reagan declared that there was a debt crisis in the country. By the time he left office he had increased that debt by nearly $3 billion due to his tax cuts to the wealthy. His successor, George H.W. Bush, despite his campaign pledge to "read my lips" and not raise taxes, knew all along he would need to if he wanted to balance the budget—which probably doomed his re-election. Despite all this, to the right wing propaganda machine, Ronald Reagan is touted as a hero in fiscal responsibility.

And then Clinton carried on with the Reagan Revolution, cutting welfare programs. As people were kicked off welfare, poverty increased while the rich got richer.

Even worse for the American worker, he signed the free-trade bill, The North Atlantic Free Trade Agreement (NAFTA), that offshored millions of good paying American jobs so corporations could exploit Mexican workers. Third party candidate Ross Perot warned about a "giant sucking sound" as jobs left the country. Why did Clinton carry on with Reagan policies? Because he was in the clutches of transnational corporations.

He launched a bloody war in Kosovo, espousing crimes of "ethnic cleansing", referring to the purge of Albanians. In fact, the Albanians and Serbians had been squabbling for centuries. The NATO invasion with air strikes and incredible suffering that ensued for the Serbian people continues to this day, all because Clinton wanted to appease the military industrialists.

He signed a bill rescinding the Glass-Steagall Act, which allowed financial speculators to gamble with the savings of Americans, which led like the shot of an arrow to the banking crisis in 2007/2008.

As of this writing, President Obama has decided to leave it to the next administration on whether or not to allow the KXL pipeline to be built, which shows what grass roots activism can accomplish, since allowing it would be a huge PR problem for the president and reelecting a Democrat in 2016. However, part of the pipeline has already been built in anticipation of it going through.

The mining of the tar sands in Canada is the most destructive and polluting means of extraction there is. First, they clear the land and then strip mine it, draining out a slurry tar-like substance that has to be mixed with horribly toxic chemicals to liquefy it. They would then ship this sludge to the United States for refining. Why don't they do the refining and shipping in Canada? Because Canadian law doesn't allow such environmentally damaging processes, and they want to send it to the United States which supposedly doesn't have such laws. In fact, it does: it's called the Clean Air Act, and Clean Water Act, signed by President Nixon, which in the past decades have been ignored by politicians when convenient for polluting corporations. The oil, coal and natural gas industries have been granted immunity from these environmental laws. After it is refined, it will not be used in the United States to unburden us from foreign oil as their propaganda claims, but to be sent to the Gulf of Mexico and exported for private profits.

CHAPTER 6

By 2008, most of FDR's socialistic programs had been rescinded and there was an economic crash similar to what happened in 1929. This time, rather than waiting for an FDR-style New Deal to occur, the government reacted immediately to the crisis by doling out trillions of dollars to the banks. This empowered the rich, but the economy still stagnated, and millions of homeowners had their homes repossessed.

Trade laws which had grown exponentially since the passage of NAFTA, have carried on even faster under Obama, as he continues to tout a "free-market" philosophy, that is not free at all, but regulated to put more money into the palms of corporations. With global expansion there are no constraints of U.S. labor laws, economic standards, and health, safety, or environmental regulations. The transnationals have what they wanted, an unrestrained market with unlimited profit. They are able to avoid taxes, skirt regulations, and pollute to their heart's content—their only expenses the millions they spend on lobbying and campaign contributions which are more than adequately made up in profits.

And as Obama continues to push trade laws in Central America, South Korea, and now the southern hemisphere of the Pacific, worker exploitation and extraction of resources continues unrestrained with neoliberal, or neoclassical, or neoconservative (pick your poison) economic polices

American democracy has been co-opted by psychopathic globalists. As a result, thousands of American manufacturing plants have been shut down and millions of Americans have lost their good-paying jobs. Go to any rural area in this country and what you will find is mass unemployment, people surviving on welfare, or work "under the table," bartering, drug dealing, etc. In the major cities corporations such as Amazon, Microsoft, Apple, Boeing, General Dynamics thrive and pay good money to their execs, a pittance to their workers, while in the rest of the city for the most part exists a service economy, which now includes non-union truck drivers, small-time manufacturing and small businesses that cannot afford to pay a living wage to their employees since they are barely getting by themselves. And they are all forced to shop at Walmart.

In Seattle, symptomatic of a shift in the mood of the electorate, an admitted socialist was elected to the city

council, Kshama Suwant, which has made the rest of the council anxious despite the majority hold they still have. Fed up with a council that has kowtowed to the city's elite in terms of sports stadiums and overdevelopment without an infrastructure to support it, and despite the "democratic" will of the people, Suwant looks at housing development as a means to provide housing for the needy, not to make some greedy developer richer.

Suwant has called for Boeing's workers to take over the factories, which of course is a Marxist concept, with the workers controlling the means of production, similar to what REI, PCC and Southwest Airlines do—all successful companies with no billionaires aboard. Boeing blackmailed the workers into giving up their hard earned pensions and other benefits, threatening to offload the production of the new 777 if they didn't. James McNerney, the recently retired CEO of Boeing, has a pension of approximately $58.5 million* from the same pension trust that has been taken away from Boeing's workers. That's free-market capitalism, folks. Gotta love it.

*Industrial News

CHAPTER 7

To add to all the other economic issues that are threatening our existence are plastics, chemical toxins invented in the lab by scientists hired for corporate interests that are leaching into our environment, and will continue to do so for—from our fragile viewpoint—forever.

Soccer balls, basketballs, and footballs that all used to be made out of leather are now made of plastic. Our clothing, our shoes, our furniture, our upholstery—now made up of mostly plastics. Our vehicles are half plastic, the interior, the bumpers, the taillight covers. We once used wood fountain pens that were refilled with environmentally friendly ink. The pen I was using when I began writing this chapter in longhand is a cheap plastic Bic that when empty I will toss into the garbage and grab another. Does anybody buy pens anymore? They just seem to be here, omnipresent, appearing like magic, littering our streets. Even rubber bands are no longer made from rubber.

PVC is one of the most toxic substances there are. Black oil is mixed with chemicals and formed to last forever—of course it won't; nothing does—but when it decomposes it contaminates the environment with toxins. How these incredibly toxic chemicals are produced is a corporate propriety secret. Plastic water bottles, which are omnipresent around the globe, leach chemicals into the contained water, compromising our health. Scratches on the bottle are the beginning of decomposition. Heat, oxygen and time all add to the decomposition.

Ships, cargo and otherwise, regularly and illegally toss their garbage into the ocean. A piece of floating plastic looks appetizing to fish. They eat it, get sick—die.

Baby bottles used to be made of glass. Now they are made of plastic. The nipples that used to be rubber are now plastic. The chemicals from the bottle leach into the baby formula. Babies gnaw on the nipple. The baby grows up with these chemicals in his/her body, developing possible serious health problems.

If you were to have a blood sample taken and tested for plastics, you would find these chemicals in your bloodstream. These chemicals cause infertility (which may not be a bad thing, come to think of it), various sicknesses, organic damage, and possibly cancer.

It is obvious that plastic in our environment is harmful, but just how harmful we don't know since it hasn't been around long enough to know for sure, for just a few decades. But the amount of plastics in our environment keeps increasing, despite our recycling efforts and environment consciousness, a consciousness that mostly doesn't exist worldwide. Some scientists believe plastic in our environment is a more threatening issue to society than global warming.

A class revolution is necessary to eliminate plastics from our environment, a monumental task obviously, since they have become so omnipresent. The keyboard I am typing right now is plastic. Just for fun, pay attention to how much plastic you purchase or use on a daily basis. Next time you go to Costco, look at the packaging, which practically requires a chain saw to get open.

CHAPTER 8

Thomas Jefferson said that every generation should have a kind of revolution, responding to the particular welfare and needs of the times, such as the proliferation of guns, for one palpable example. There have been about twelve generations since he said that, and for a time these revolutions did indeed occur.

Jefferson was concerned about the clear-cutting land of trees, knowing it would deleteriously affect future generations. He believed that current generations needed to nurture the earth for the sake of future generations.

He believed that even the laws enshrined in our Constitution should be subject to changes according to the current needs, the laws needing to change accordingly. He believed that the current Constitution needed to expire at the latest after 34 years, examined, and changed if necessary to adapt to current needs. In short, Jefferson was saying that in order for America to advance, so must its laws.

Second amendment fanatics take note.

He said this because of what he believed to be flaws in our Constitution. He noted that a rigid Constitution was no different than a dictatorship. He said we needed to adapt and alter the constitution in order to abide to current conditions.

Yeah, yeah, I know what you're thinking: "Jefferson had slaves!"

Indeed, Jefferson had slaves. He had a slave as a mistress, and he was terrible with finances, leaving his estate bankrupt when he died. He believed Blacks and Native Americans were subhuman. Yes, like all of us, he was flawed. But let's for at least the moment forget his flaws and take note of his brilliance—which was immense.

Mountain climbers today don't wear the same climbing outfits as George Mallory did, and nor should the Constitution be cut in stone.

Jefferson lived in an era of government during which almost half of our forefathers were calling for a monarchy similar to the one they had fought a war against. John Adams, elected in 1796, began to move in that direction. Jefferson's party was the Democratic Republicans, as opposed to Adam's Federalist Party, and Jefferson practically singlehandedly prevented the country from becoming a monarchy. Jefferson called this a revolution.

The next "revolution" came in 1820 with the election of Andrew Jackson. He even campaigned on overturning the existing order, taking on the Second Bank of the United States, vetoing their renewal of the charter. He was considered a hero by many Americans for taking on the rich and powerful.

Thirty years after that came Abraham Lincoln and the Civil War, launching another revolution, this time a bloody one, the bloodiest in American history. With it came the Emancipation Proclamation.

In 1880 there was another revolution, taking on the Robber Barons of the railroads, steel and finance. This was called the "Gilded Age."

In 1907 the revolution came with Teddy Roosevelt, who also took on the rich and powerful. He also curtailed the clear-cutting of land by creating national parks. He signed the Tillman Act, which prevented corporations from bribing federal officials.

The next revolution occurred in 1932 when FDR was elected. He launched the New Deal in response to the Great Depression, providing federal dollars to put people back to work, and created a social security system so that retired people had a guaranteed pension.

The next revolution came in 1961 with the election of John Fitzgerald Kennedy. He too took on the rich corporations, exemplified most prominently in the Military Industrial Complex, which his predecessor Dwight D.

Eisenhower had warned us about in his retirement speech when he told us about the social programs that could be created from the cost of one battle ship.

The Kennedy brothers were eliminated, which was essentially a coup d'état, and with it came an end to generational revolutions. Every president since JFK has been pawn to the unbridled power of the military/corporate plutocracy. LBJ saw how hopeless it was to carry on with JFK's legacy, and before launching a campaign for re-election, resigned in disgrace, despite his gains in Civil Rights legislation.

The reins of power were handed over to Richard Nixon, who was more that happy to carry on with the military/corporate agenda. So did Jimmy Carter, though not so eagerly. He simply hadn't the character, will, or power to take it on. He asked the citizenry to sacrifice, but not the major corporations. He became a better human being as a private citizen.

Ronald Reagan called his administration a revolution, but that was an oxymoron. It was a call for laissez-faire capitalism, giving even more power to the corporations with even more stifling of democracy. He called his economic policy "supply-side" saying that by giving more money to the rich, money would rain down on the populace like candy.

The Reagan Revolution was a direct response to the Movement of the 60s, the anti-war, pro-environment movement that had idolized JFK, RFK and MLK and was the current generational revolution, a revolution that failed miserably. Reagan also for the most part shut down any pro-environment gains made by Nixon and Carter, using a sixties slogan.

Socialist activists such as Michael Harrington (JFK had consulted him), and ecologists such as Rachael Carson and back to the land movements led by Scott and Helen Nearing, and consumer activists such as Ralph Nader were all for the most part reeled in and rendered ineffective in responding to corporate power with their own brands of revolution.

The crash of 2008 was about twenty years after Reagan, just in time for Thomas Jefferson's revolution, which came in the form of the Occupy Movement, but it too was shut down by the power structure, and President Obama despite his rhetoric of support, behind the scenes worked tirelessly for the interests of the corporation.

And the Tea Party that emerged from the era of George W. Bush made up of primarily baby boomers, carried on with the radical free-enterprise movement. In fact, they weren't radical at all; they were far right reactionaries, wanting to reverse the progressive gains of FDR that had made their lives comfortable. This is the irony of the movement, since it was the baby boomers who were the primary beneficiaries of the New Deal, as the Tea Party tried to unravel it. The ignorance of this grass-roots movement was exemplified with one Tea Party member exclaiming that the government better keep its hands off his Medicare.

The Supreme Court's ruling on Citizen's United resulted in that which Jefferson feared most about the budding democracy: The turning of the country into a monarchy of corporate rule, that monarchy represented in the unbridled power of Supreme Court Justice John Roberts.

In Citizen's United v Federal Election Commission, the Supreme Court ruled in favor of Citizen's United, giving constitutional personhood to corporations.

This ruling was reinforced in 2014 with McClutcheon v Federal Election Commission when the Supreme Court ruled that there was no limit an individual could contribute to a political party. These rulings expanded plutocracy rule of the rich over the rest of us. It will mean that major corporations will have even more influence over a Democratic Party that traditionally had populist roots, empowering the Democratic Party's neoliberal wing—the ideological heroes of the Clinton era, which in 2016 will most likely be represented by Hillary Clinton as president.

CHAPTER 9

The philosophy behind hedge fund trading is to allow individuals or financial institutions to push worthless investments and then bet that they will fail. This philosophy was used in the subprime mortgage scam, which encouraged Americans to buy mortgages that the banks knew they wouldn't be able to pay off, so that the banks could foreclose on them and then flip them. This came to a head in 2008, when the American taxpayer rescued these failed banks. The billionaires got richer, and millions of Americans lost their homes.

As a result of this economic pyramid scheme, in-debt nations in Europe were encouraged to adopt "austerity" measures. People were thrown off government social programs that had become a progressive part of their lives, as well as pensions, health care, etc. Wages and benefits were cut. Unemployment increased. The worst-case scenario of this was in Greece, where mass protests broke out, there and around the world, including the Occupy Movement and the Arab Spring.

Goldman Sachs and other top financial organizations performed a global coup d'état. As the global economy went under, Goldman Sachs got richer. In essence, this was a global hedge fund scam. The world economy that used to be an economy of working people now became an economy of financial investment, creating trillions of dollars for the rich while the people suffered, lost their homes, lost their pensions, benefits and other social benefits that were the basis of European social welfare. Greece, Ireland, Spain, and Portugal took it in the shorts while the billionaires got richer. The one country that refused to engage in this austerity scam was Iceland, having learned their lesson in the previous shock doctrine, neoliberal scam, and not about to go through it again, isolating themselves from the rest of Europe, and doing just fine on their own, thank you very much, with their sensibly restrained population of 350,000, accompanied by a strict immigration policy.

What was done in Europe was also done in the United States in places like Detroit and Wisconsin, with people losing their jobs and pensions. Boeing threatened to leave Seattle unless the unions agreed to surrender their guaranteed pensions and cuts in health care and received massive tax breaks from the state, putting more burden on the working class to maintain infrastructure. Scott Walker in Wisconsin and Rick Snyder in Michigan instituted their own austerity measures, cutting people's benefits and pensions.

All over the country we have witnessed cutbacks in services such as police, prisons, fire, schools, transit, etc., in a conspiratorial move to purge all public programs and privatize everything. The charter school movement is nothing more than a scam for taxpayers to fund private schools, at the sacrifice of public schools. The infrastructure crumbles, as there is no money for repairs. And then the people blame the state for not maintaining it.

And in our government, as fewer taxes are going for government programs, the corporate led media and in turn the people blame the government for problems in the IRS and the Veterans Hospitals, problems caused primarily by lack of funds.

Meanwhile, American corporations hoard trillions of dollars in overseas accounts. As they stimulate the stock market with worthless financial speculation, they set us up for another financial collapse. The European banks are doing the same. According to the Institute of International Finance, the U.S., Great Britain, the Eurozone, and France are sitting on $8 trillion in cash. The wealthiest people on the planet have as much as $32 trillion stored in overseas financial institutions, according to the *Justice Network*. Money News reported that American companies are quietly dumping their American stocks, which includes such so-called "liberals" as George Soros, Bill Gates, and Warren Buffett.

According to a Senator Elizabeth Warren, they even do this illegally. The laws are "too complex for the very regulators who are supposed to monitor them."

And the federal deficit continues to grow needlessly.

CHAPTER 10

After World War II, the United States helped Japan and Germany develop a manufacturing base, which created a strong middle class in both countries. Both these countries also implemented labor protections and benefits, and a social safety net stronger than in the United States. They developed a high-speed train system, and they did it all while giving decent wages and benefits to their workers.

In Obama's State of the Union Address, he stated he was going to lead the country into a green industrial economy, committed to giving "eighty percent of Americans access to high speed rail."

Trains would help end our dependence on oil while providing a cheap source for transportation. Trains now have magnetized-levitation technology that never touches the grid. They use no coal, electricity or any traditional power source at all. Yet up till now, no plans exist to create a high-speed rail system. High-speed rail systems in Europe and Asia run along at 200 miles per hour. Amtrak trains, by contrast, while costing about twice as much as the average European train, plod along at a top speed of 70 miles per hour, at an expense few can afford.

Cars, buses, and planes rule America's transportation system, putting more CO_2 into the atmosphere than any other country but China. And Obama's $89.2 billion request for rail is a ridiculously small amount needed to meet his rhetorical call for Americans to have access to high-speed rail. A genuine commitment to high-speed rail would not only be good for the environment, it would create jobs in construction and mass transit, but the Republicans and Democrats are obviously too stymied by the right-wing power structure, succumbing to the interests of the oil and gas industries, as they continue to allow fracking and its demonizing effect on the environment and communities.

Germany today, unlike most of the rest of Europe, is well off, with a huge government surplus and trade surplus, all the while still giving their workers decent pay and benefits. Germans pride themselves on their industriousness and don't feel sympathetic to countries like Greece for not pulling themselves up by the bootstraps, instead relying too much on government handouts. They only reluctantly agreed to give up the mark and join the Eurozone and were not enthusiastic about bailing out the rest of Europe. So rather than embarking on something similar to the Marshall Plan that the U.S. adopted after World War II, they expanded the financial crisis by demanding that the rest of Europe adopt austerity measures in exchange for bailing them out. They loaned money to Portugal, Greece, Spain and Ireland and demanded that embrace austerity measures, cutting wages, benefits, and social programs.

And today, the U.S. is involved in military action throughout the Arab world, in Afghanistan, Iraq, Yemen, Libya, Somalia, Pakistan, and God knows where else. Nearly half of our tax dollars goes to the military. Besides the many who have died in these military misadventures, a good portion of the men who return from war are damaged physically and mentally. In 2012 a record number of men and women in the military committed suicide. War also causes soldiers to lose their sense of morality, oftentimes resorting to torturing prisoners and taking this deranged attitude home to their friends and spouses, many of them becoming police officers. And now the people at home are practically immune to it, having gotten used to the use of torture in the Bush administration and now the use of drones in the Obama administration.

Between 1997 and 2012 the defense budget soared. Besides dispensing death, destruction and horror, war dispenses waste. One bomb can cost $100 million. Once it is dropped it leaves horror and devastation and is worth nothing.

Obviously, much of military spending is a wasteful use of money that could be put into health care, schools, infrastructure, to name just a few. Drone strikes are just adding to the problem: we murder innocent people that enrage Muslims, who then join fringe groups we call "terrorists." Someone in the Arab world was quoted as saying: "For every 10 Islamists that are killed, 500 rise to take their place."

In 1803 right wing Federalist Chief Justice John Marshall said in a case Marbury v Madison that the Supreme Court could strike down laws that were unconstitutional. Up until then, the Supreme Court was the weakest of the three branches of government. With that ruling, it became the strongest; a tribunal that virtually became a monarchy. John Marshall had, in essence, declared himself a king, with the ability to oust laws that Congress had passed but the Court determined were unconstitutional.

Thomas Jefferson was appalled, declaring that the Supreme Court "now could twist and shape the constitution to any form they pleased."

He was unable to get any momentum from Congress to pass any laws limiting the power of the Supreme Court.

This ruling has carried on into our modern era, with decisions such as Citizens United and the McClutcheon ruling. With this power they have essentially created the monarchy that the Federalists wanted. In 2000, they declared George W. Bush president, stopping a recount in

Florida that would have given the presidency to Al Gore. And in 2004, electronic voting machines re-elected him.

In 2009, a study by Harvard University found that 45 million Americans were without health care. After World War II, when the warring nations began to heal, one of these repairs was in health care, instituting a single payer system, ensuring it through taxation. Nearly every industrial country did this—except the United States. Nearly every president since FDR tried to implement some form of government sponsored health care. LBJ managed to implement Medicare, but for the most part, corporate power has stymied any implementation of a government sponsored health care system. Obamacare ensures that our taxes continue to support the private health insurance companies.

Today, when you turn 65 you are required to apply for Medicare, whether you take it or not. If you take it, and most of us will need to, a certain percentage is taken out of your Social Security check to pay for it, even though you have been paying into it your entire working career, or at least since LBJ signed it into law. And then it only covers 80%, so you are forced to purchase supplemental insurance, which can cost hundreds of dollars a month to get the coverage that the elderly need, and even then it has deductibles and co-pays and doesn't cover eyeglasses and dental. At an age when nearly all of us will need these two items, we have to pay for them ourselves.

As the cost of health care skyrockets, Medicare is woefully insufficient. The Affordable Health Care has helped some, hurt others, but nonetheless, it too is woefully insufficient. Medicare has parts A, B, C and D—but it needs a Part E, to cover "Everybody, " free of cost. Canada has such a system; even so does Mexico.

Today, the Veterans Administration is under attack for its lack of proper care. Like the IRS, Social Security, and Medicare, these problems are due to a lack of money. Corporate power is conspiring to make government programs look bad so that privatization is implemented. It is happening today in addition to health care in prisons, schools, police, fire, and infrastructure, and the Democrats are going right along with it.

Money put into health care would relieve immense burden on American families, preventing deaths and bankruptcies. Investments into our economy, into infrastructure, into green energy, would put people to work and help the nation and help heal the world.

CHAPTER 11

The last thirty years has seen a decimation of organized labor and with it the middle class. With this decimation we have seen the rise of a powerful oligarchy. As the average workers have seen their standard of living decreasing, the wealth of the rich has skyrocketed.

Because the super rich have taken control of our three branches of government, the working class is now powerless to do anything about it. Even their vote is meaningless as they are forced time after time to vote for the lesser of two evils. Municipalities too kowtow to the demagogue as hugely profitable companies such as Boeing, Microsoft, and Amazon make demands for huge tax breaks or threaten to leave town. So Democrats and Republicans alike submit to their demands, and the burden of taxation is put on the working class. In Washington State, even so-called "liberals" Governor Jay Inslee and Senator Patty Murray have sacrificed the livelihood of working people to satisfy the sociopathic greed of the local corporations, by giving them ever more tax breaks.

In 2008, the Democrats had a majority in Congress and a Democrat for president. What did they do to exploit this opportunity to increase the living standards of working people? They passed trade laws that exported more American jobs so that corporations could exploit slave labor overseas and extract more resources from the "third world" for private profits. They expanded oil and coal industry interests in fracking, offshore drilling, and mountain top removal—all of which destroys land, pollutes water, and damages the health of communities. They bailed out the banks when the world economy was about to go under. They continued to give huge tax breaks to major corporations. They gave nearly half of our taxes to the military industrialists. That's our Democratic Party, the "people's" party, the party of FDR.

As every rational economist will tell you, the best way to stimulate the economy is to put people to work. Work gives people money, which they then spend in a cycle of monetary exchange. This stimulation does *not* include investment in the stock market, where actually monetary exchange stops—into the hands of the rich, who simply collect this money to become richer. They don't put it into the economy—at least not anymore.

Contrary to what Mitt Romney and the other far right conservatives say, the rich are not "job creators." They are in fact parasites, sucking the earth of resources, exploiting the workers, and polluting the environment to increase their wealth. They are so psychotic in this endeavor that they think that they are securing their future as if they are going to live forever. They put their money in offshore accounts to avoid paying taxes. Congress could do something about it, but instead they enable the process. Because of corporations' obsessive, shortsighted greed, they have actually conspired to put the planet and most of its inhabitants on the verge of extinction.

The latest report from the UN about the inevitable consequences of climate change is almost redundant. We have known about the consequences for decades now, and virtually nothing has been done. For years now Earth has been experiencing increased droughts, flooding and increasing violent storms as a result of global warming. When we had our chances to reverse the process, our leaders instead ignored the warnings of leading ecologists and biologists and instead bowed to the interests of Wall Street. Our leaders talk about more efficient cars, tax incentives, recycling, etc., but still allow the major causes of climate change to exist: drilling for oil, coal, agribusiness, fracking, and nuclear—all for the sake of private profits, not energy independence. Many experts now say it's too late too stop it; the tipping point has passed. The technology exists for us to switch completely to renewables, but we are stymied by a world still controlled by parasitic capitalism.

Burning of oil and coal products is the primary contributors to climate change, and they continue to be the primary source of the world's energy. The world's richest countries continue to be so because of oil. And if they don't share these oil profits with energy companies, they become enemies. Iran, Iraq, Venezuela are all, or were, enemies because they had nationalized their oil.

PART TWO

MARX AND MARXISM

CHAPTER 1

To the political left of the world, Karl Marx is undoubtedly the most influential economic philosopher of all time, as well as the most misunderstood and misinterpreted. From the right, he is the most maligned, nothing less than the devil incarnate, promoter of a philosophy that creates the biggest threat to the free exchange of capital and the establishment of individual freedom, happiness, and well-being.

In truth, Karl Marx developed his economic philosophy on the puppet strings of other economic theorists. Communism as a theory was already well entrenched before Karl Max was born. He himself was constantly altering his own particular philosophy his whole life, developing and evolving, and when he died his third volume of *Capital* lay unfinished, a pile of messy notes that his friend and closest partner Frederick Engels had to go through and delineate, putting in much of his own philosophy in place of Marx's.

Contemporary economic orthodoxy of the so-called neoclassical economic theorists have dismissed Marx as old-fashioned and untenable, using the Soviet Union,

China and Cuba as convenient examples, while his proponents point out that Marx's economic predictions have manifested themselves in the regularly recurring economic crises endemic to capitalism. The difference is that Karl Marx died frustrated and disillusioned that these constant crises that occurred over and over never resulted in the inevitable revolution he expected during his lifetime.

He was most disappointed with the result of the people's revolution in 1848 against the French monarchy. Almost as soon as the old order collapsed, the revolution fell apart, as the bourgeoisie became alarmed by what the working class was demanding, and the conservatives took advantage and were able to reinstate new forms of dictatorship.

We can see these patterns repeating themselves today worldwide, as revolutions in places such as Libya, Syria, Egypt, Iraq and elsewhere have responded to their impoverishment only to be co-opted by world powers that reinstate dictatorships that cater to world economic power. And the strongest military power in the world, the United States, keeps enabling this with unending military support, which actually is support of the military industrialists.

In France in 1848, an organized workers movement led by Marx and many other socialist leaders demanded radical economic liberalization and social changes. Liberals wanted more restraint, and joined forces with the conservatives, seeing authoritarianism as the lesser of two evils, much the same as we do every four years in the United States, the result of which we perpetually succumb to a fascist system that supports the corporate elite.

Karl Marx's philosophical reflections for the most part began as a university student in the League of Poets, a group of young men who met to discuss literary and aesthetic questions, made up of mostly literary types wanting to be poets and novelists. And Marx's primary activities were drinking and brawling in the German pubs, which seem more like the antics of a late-blooming adolescent than a future philosophical icon. Still, dissent resonated among these rowdy students against Prussian rule. Between the drinking, brawling, and duels that Marx engaged in, he became fascinated with the ideas of philosopher Georg Wilhelm Friedrich Hegel, an extremely complex and convoluted philosopher, who in turn dovetailed his ideas from the eighteenth-century German philosopher Emmanuel Kant. Hegel would have a monumental impact on the formation of Marx's philosophies, on which a subject's consciousness of the objective world would be transformed into an expanded version of self-consciousness. This self-consciousness would evolve throughout human history Darwinian-like, of which Hegel would call the "Abstract Spirit" or "Mind." This systematic, organizing body of knowledge which the Germans called "Wissenschaft"

would manifest itself in the natural world and such as in the evolution of law, politics, and government.

While to many of us today, this may seem obscure and terribly intellectual, to Marx and his contemporaries it had huge impact, and Hegelism became for these students who were rebelling against the doctrines of organized religion, almost a religion itself.

When Marx proudly wrote home to his father Heinrich about these enlightening ideas, his father predictably wrote back that these philosophical musings were useless for furthering his life's career. As Marx's life unfolded, this prediction would certainly turn out to be true, from a financially secure viewpoint. He and his ever-expanding family would be in perpetual financial straights their whole lives. He would have to be repeatedly rescued by Frederick Engels, his good friend and near intellectual equal. An argument could be made that Engels enabled his friend, since when Marx had money he was not frugal with it. The man who would write *the Communist Manifesto* was a spendthrift.

As Marx's financial woes mounted, he became bitter about his mother's refusal to give him an advance on the inheritance he felt he deserved now rather than after her death. His mother, on the other hand, thought her son should instead be obtaining gainful employment. There is obvious irony in the fact that Marx demanded money that in essence wasn't his to begin with to provide for the bourgeois existence he philosophized against. This of course gives ammunition to right wing theory that those who receive money they don't earn are deadbeats.

As an example of Marx's improvident ways, when Marx was newly wed to Jenny, the bride's mother provided them with honeymoon money that was supposed to last until Karl got a job. They went through it all in two weeks. Marx was freely handing out money to friends and acquaintances without expecting to be paid back. We've all known people like this, but it's behavior usually reserved to nincompoops, sociopaths, or narcissists—not to those of a methodical mind like Karl Marx. He was even bitter that Jenny was not provided with a proper dowry—perhaps a common expectation then—but still, money that wouldn't have been his to begin with. Astonishingly, Marx apparently believed that money should be tossed about without budgetary restraint. What did he expect would happen when it came time to pay the rent or put food on the table?

Apparently, he spent his whole life believing that his philosophical musings were lofty enough to be deserving of monetary compensation. Frederick Engels obliged this philosophy over and over, no doubt keeping Marx out of debtor's prison and his family out of the poor house. The famous writer James Joyce had the same attitude, and spending habits, believing that because he was a genius who had written (in his mind) the greatest novel in literary history, he was entitled to financial compensation, regardless of whether people purchased his masterpiece or not. Joyce too had a wealthy admirer who fulfilled this duty. Genius does have its rewards.

As an editor for the *Rhineland News*, Marx courted liberal members of the bourgeoisie. He actually wrote a number of editorials in favor of free trade and denouncing protectionism, a position that must confuse leftists of today who oppose global free trade. Even after he became a communist, he would continue to support free trade, but only because he believed it would expedite the revolution. Controversy, argument, and debate reigned among left wing thought then as much as it does today.

Marx was even critical of certain philosophies that would someday be known as "Marxism." He dismissed communism as ominous, the implementation for such ideas "defeat our intelligence and conquer our sentiments." The man who would write *The Communist Manifesto* five years hence even advanced the idea of using the military to suppress the communists' worker revolts. At the time he believed in strict Hegelian solution.

His Hegelian analysis, however, failed to provide any solutions for the poor. That would have to evolve. Marx's initial philosophy about the basic social question moved vaguely along the lines of capitalist thought and free-market liberalism—much like the neoliberal economists of today such as Thomas Friedman. However, unlike Friedman and his ilk, who have complete faith in government, there was animosity toward authoritarian Prussian rule, which Marx accented in his editorials. Today's neoliberal elites, at least in the mainstream press, such as the *New York Times*, have complete faith in our plural political system. To have no other choice than to vote for either a Democrat or Republican is pure democracy in action to these editors, most if not all of whom are wealthy. Friedman in fact is a billionaire.

CHAPTER 2

Marx looked to France as the country that would first achieve his predicted socialist revolution. He was an admirer of Jean-Jacques Rousseau, having underlined passages in *Social Contract*. Marx's ideas of the general interest of the social body under a democratic regime were similar to Rousseau's concepts.

The entire gamut from left to right politics was present in French political discussions, from pro-conservatism to anti-government liberalism, to radical democrats and republicans, to pacifist Flourier socialists, to revolutionary communists. Unlike the mainstream world press today, the press in France freely printed all these voices. There were parliamentary debates, legal and clandestine associations, public and private gatherings. Marx looked outside Prussia to France for the social and political circles that seemed to have freedom of expression. It is very likely that Paris played a major role in shaping Marx's future writings. Marx moved his family there in 1843

Combined with Hegel's philosophy of the Absolute Spirit and the French radicals' and socialists' criticisms of post-revolutionary order in France, Marx's acquaintance with the proletariat, with its suffering, struggles and aspirations, caused his revolutionary ideas to evolve in leaps and bounds. Here began his thoughts that human freedom involved an end to capitalism. Even though Marx was a Jew, he began to identify capitalism with the Jews in a derogatory manner, and many critics of Marx would come to identify Marx as an anti-Semite. This propaganda would be expanded decades later with the Bolsheviks and what would become the Soviet Union and their persecution of Jews. Marx, certainly, was not absent of prejudice, and probably carried commonly held beliefs at that time of Aryan superiority over all races. It was common among the German liberal Protestant theologians to condemn Jewish economic practices as self-interested, immoral, and exploitive—the common complaint about capitalism of course, and it was seen then that it was the Jew in general who most exploited capitalism, their success endemic to their race. It was like blaming immigrants for immigration.

Despite his innate prejudices, Marx believed that a transformation to a socialist democracy included Jews—and everyone else. To make a point, Marx turned to a unpredictable example: the United States, where according to the writer Alexis de Tocqueville, a multitude of religions flourished freely, exclusive in a secular state. The founders of the American Constitution included in the First Amendment among its freedoms the freedom of religion. The emancipation of Jews was part of the creation of a democratic state. Unfortunately, he didn't stop himself there and went on to refer to the "worldly cult" of Jews with their "haggling and bargaining." Marx believed in the democratic emancipation of Jews, but he identified Jews with the evils of capitalism. Marx's philosophical flaw here was avoiding the reality that in order to survive in a capitalist society, one has to be a capitalist, including himself, the one who was bitter with his mother for not advancing his inheritance and perpetually depended on Engels for money to keep from starving.

Another contradiction to the communist committed to the proletariat was his continual pursuit to live like a bourgeoisie and his association with the bourgeoisies. He encouraged his daughters to have suitable husbands, which meant husbands who could take care of them financially, and was disappointed when they followed the example of their mother and married radicals.

CHAPTER 3

Marx and Engels believed that humans distinguished themselves from animals when they began to produce their means of subsistence, rather than devouring it, which produces indirectly their material life. Humans were human through their collective production, their working together to produce what they needed from nature. This was the "commune" in "communism." This was all part of advancing technology, economic organization, and the fair division of labor. This material production determined ideas, culture, law, and politics—all united under the concept of ideology. Marx and Engels evolved from the Young Hegelians, criticizing them for creating ideas, rather than practical situations that would move history forward. The most profound, and possibly most difficult part of this philosophy for the individual to accept, was that communal ownership meant the elimination of private property. All property would become part of the commons. For those who have owned and nurtured home and land, this is near impossible to accept, and was of course a major criticism of the Bolshevist revolution, which was brilliantly espoused in Boris Pasternak's novel *Doctor Zhivago*.

Marx and Engels envisioned a society in which industries would engage in labor that they enjoy, working on tasks that appealed to them: those who liked to work with wood would become carpenters or furniture makers; those who were interested in medicine would become doctors, and so forth. No one, ideally, would have to labor at that which they didn't like. Obviously, this drew skeptical response. Who would want to be a ditch digger, for example? Such a society would be utopian, and as such, a pipe dream, not reality.

In 1848 and 1849 Marx became a revolutionary. His editorials in the *Rhineland News* were brash and subversive, repeatedly encouraging and fomenting revolution. He pushed for a democratic revolution to destroy the autocratic Prussian monarchy. Marx repeatedly looked to the French revolution as an example. A popular slogan that has been incorrectly attributed to Marx emerged: "Workers of the world unite!" A first draft of *The Communist Manifesto* began to be serialized by Marx and Engels just as revolutionary fever was already spreading through Europe. During this time, Marx encouraged capitalist free trade as a feature that would make the inevitable revolution more imminent. Most socialists preached protectionism, then as now, as a rejection of the primary free market.

In 1847, the League of Congress assigned Marx the task of writing the organization's political platform. What resulted was a literary masterwork, *The Communist Manifesto*. It defined the historical progression and inevitable victory of the proletariat. An increasingly crisis-ridden capitalism had created an even larger, more impoverished proletariat, which would lead them to revolution. "May the ruling class tremble at the thought of a communist revolution," he concluded with bluster. "The proletarians have nothing to lose in that revolution but their chains. They have a world to gain."

The *Manifesto* also praised the bourgeoisie's highly revolutionary role, calling for them to tear down the existing social, economic, and intellectual system to build its own, characterized by ceaseless change.

History has shown this to not work out as prophesized, in view of the rise of Nationalism in pre-1914 Europe, the nightmare of World War I, and again with the rise of the Nazis and World War II. Here in 2015 it has yet to happen, though it has oftentimes been attempted, with the capitalists always managing to overcome it, in Europe, Latin America, Africa, and of course in North America. Devoted Marxists still point to *The Communist Manifesto* as prophecy, insisting after 150 years it still must happen if working people are to be free. True perhaps, but time is a significant worry at this point: the ice caps are melting. And

Marx's idea that global trade would facilitate revolution certainly seems to have credence today, as labor has been reduced world-wide to its lowest common denominator.

Nevertheless, no sooner had *The Communist Manifesto* left the printing presses then revolution broke out in France in February 1848.

At this time Marx's whereabouts is unknown by historians, and it might seem that Marx had fled in panic from the revolution he had encouraged. Another criticism of Marx is that while he himself called for violent revolution, he did not put himself into the midst of it. In other words, he was accused of being a coward.

In the end, the government was taken control by Louis Napoleon Bonaparte, a near repeat of what happened in the French revolution of 1789, when in 1793 his famous uncle had taken power. A restoration of the monarchy seemed imminent. The new French government was even offering to send their armies to Italy to overthrow the Roman Republic and reinstate the Pope. Tens of thousands of leftists stormed the streets in protest. Expecting another violent revolution, the conservative government responded with a violent show of force, dispersing the demonstrators and arresting leftist leaders. There was good reason for Marx's hiding, if that's what he was doing: the government was threatening to arrest him. His position in Paris was increasingly precarious. Marx and his family fled to London, where he would live the rest of his life.

Most of Marx's political collaborators also moved to the British Isles. Though Great Britain was technically a monarchy, and probably the greatest imperialist country in the world at that time, he found he could at least express himself and write with freedom. His main problem was the high cost of living, increasing his omnipresent financial woes. This was Dickens' London, after all. All the while, in central Europe there was growing repression and counterrevolution, increasing Marx's depression and disillusionment, as he continued to carry on bravely with clandestine political statements.

The 1848 radicals of the Prussian and German National Assemblies were calling for political and socioeconomic programs that would attempt to make the workers lives more bearable. But it would not lead to the abolition of private property and the eradication of social classes as Marx and Engels were preaching for. These reforms would delay the revolution, much like what FDR's New Deal would do nearly a century later, when the Great Depression was threatening revolution in the United States. From the safe haven of Great Britain, Marx was still calling for a violent revolution.

Meanwhile, Marx's family continued to be mired in debt. In order to maintain the middle-class lifestyle he strived for, which included a housekeeper and governess, he was forced to keep borrowing. There were embarrassing episodes with Marx begging for money from those who knew he would probably never be able to pay them back. He again wrote to his mother begging for more of his inheritance in advance. They ran up tabs with shopkeepers and pubs, the later where Marx continued to drink and socialize, with their landlady, and with anyone else who would give them credit. Many felt obligated to enable him because he was a great intellect; others did not, probably aware of his imprudent spending when he had money.

The political defeat of the 1848 rebellion increased the bitterness of their impoverished lives. But it only seemed to increase Marx's steadfast belief in the inevitable revolution.

CHAPTER 4

Marx would spend much of his time at the library or museums, studying the works of John Stuart Mill, Adam Smith, and Samuel Lloyd.

He continued to criticize the "petite-bourgeois" democrats as not revolutionary enough, a criticism which was impolitic in that many of these German communist artisans and activists in London were supporting him. Marx began pushing for violent revolution, which to many of his supporters seemed extreme and unnecessary; they felt that a social revolution could be achieved nonviolently. Marx was getting more radical as the inevitable revolution kept getting delayed.

A political divide surfaced with the Marx/Engels supporters and the Willich/Schapper communists, the later of which wanted the revolution to proceed immediately, the former willing to wait for the next economic crisis with inevitable revolution in its wake.

It should be noted here that while the Prussian government intimidated and censored leftist writings such as the *New Rhineland News*, and that Great Britain and the

United States had "freedom of the press," the truth is that censorship existed in Great Britain and even more so in the U.S. and continues to this day in the form of corporate control of the main media. While leftists were arrested and imprisoned in Prussia, in the U.S. today there are more people sitting in prison than in any other country of the world, the majority of them Black and Hispanic, and as such can be considered political prisoners. They are victims of an institutionalized racism that has existed since the founding of the country. They are denied any rights of citizenry, even after they've served their time, unable to vote, and unable to find suitable employment, which oftentimes forces them back into a life of crime, and back into prison.

Many of the Prussian prisoners were kept in solitary confinement, in dank narrow cells, with little opportunity for fresh air. These conditions were brutal, and again, the reader can be reminded that many of today's political prisoners receive similar treatment, in Guantanamo, in U.S. prisons, and in the treatment of Pfc. Bradley (now Chelsea) Manning as prime examples. If Julian Assange and Edward Snowden are extradited to the U.S. for trial, their experiences will undoubtedly be the same. The treatment of so-called subversives was the same then as now. In some ways, it's even worse now.

On December 2, 1851, Louis Napoleon Bonaparte declared himself Emperor Napoleon III, which was a severe blow to the radical exiles in London, their hopes of a renewed revolutionary upheaval centered in

France all but extinguished. But it still seemed to spur Marx on, resulting in *The Eighteenth Brumaire of Louis Bonaparte*, describing socialists and communists as the representatives of the workers, the non-communist democrats as the representatives of the petite-bourgeois, the moderate republicans and non-anarchists as representatives of certain elements of the capitalist class, and the conservatives representing large landowners. This work became a profound postmortem of the 1848 revolution, a dissertation of the failure of European revolutionary aspirations. He considered the 1848 revolution a repeat of 1789. What Marx failed to mention, however, was that the French radical politicians he mocked were devoted supporters of Karl Marx, their support enabling him to continue writing and working. His criticism of others was in essence a criticism of himself. Nevertheless, the pamphlet was inspiring to the hopes and aspirations of revolutionaries, but sadly never reached a broader audience.

Creditors continued to hound the Marx's in the 1850s. Marx's published writings paid well enough for the family to get by, but he couldn't stop his profligate spending and poor budgeting habits. Engels continued to enable Marx

when he could. They continued to rely on pawnshops and loans from others. There was a recession in the mid-50s, which added irony to their financial ills: the long-awaited economic crisis that was to lead to the inevitable revolution was further undermining family finances.

And Jenny was no better than her husband at controlling spending. Add to this, perpetual pregnancies, the children's illnesses, and Marx's physical ills. He had hemorrhoids, liver and gallbladder problems, and rotting teeth (all probably compounded by spending too much time in the pub.)

The distinguishing feature of capitalism was of its global scope, then as now, but Marx concentrated his political analyses on Europe, regarding the rest of the world subject to global imperialism by the British, Prussian, and French republics. This included the spread into America and the Orient. Marx theorized small villages, or communes, with each region working on local agriculture and craft production. This would be in response to massive industrialization and the enslavement of the proletariat. The popular regional movement of today in the form of organic food co-ops and local crafts and trades all stem from Marxist thought. Imperial rule was an integral part of the capitalist system. Marx defended the British colonization of India, but again with the idea that it would advance the revolution. It was part of his theory of historical evolution.

This expected revolution would not come to pass in Marx's lifetime, or really, ever. It wasn't until the twentieth-century when the Soviet Union, China, and Cuba would struggle to implement the ideology of Marxism, and fail, having to compete with the global rule of capitalism. These countries also refused to accept the main tenet of Marxism: that the workers control the means of production, not a centralized government. It is the major misconception of Marxism, and right-wing critics love it, their main argument of course being that there is no incentive to work when the government provides for everything. The difference is that when the workers control the business, they have incentive to make the business a success; a current example of Marxism at work is Southwest Airlines, which the employees themselves own. But nowhere in leftist rhetoric do we hear this expressed. Also, experiments in Latin America, such as Chile in the 70s with Allende and the Sandinistas in Nicaragua and elsewhere worldwide, were undermined with American imperialism, neoliberalism, covert coups, assassinations, and military power.

Disagreements among the leftists made political consensus impossible. Times haven't changed here either. Major disagreements resonated between Marx/Engels and Ferdinand Lassalle. A dramatic and flamboyant character, Lassalle was a profoundly polarizing figure. Marx disliked him for his self-centeredness and even accused him of being a spy. His silk dressing gowns and lavish apartment didn't help, which he was able to maintain through his legal work, especially by representing a Countess, Sophie von Hatzfeldt, rescuing her from an abusive husband. He brought her and her money into the left-wing circles. She provided Lassalle with a generous portion of her divorce settlement. A lot of the hostility between camps was no doubt generated from jealousy. Lassalle was not only well off, he was considered a ladies man.

Unfortunately, correspondence between Marx and Engels in regard to Lassalle was blatantly anti-Semitic. Lassalle was described as "the little Yid Braun" and "Jacob the Weasel." What they saw as Lassalle's personal faults were in terms of anti-Semite stereotypes. Despite Marx and Engel's personal antipathy toward Lassalle, they needed his financial support.

Despite their continual financial problems, the Marxes continued to pursue a bourgeois façade, which included a piano and piano lessons for their daughters. The piano teacher terminated his services when he was not paid.

Help arrived when Marx's mother died on November 30, 1862. One cannot help but wonder if Marx sighed in relief rather than grief, since he finally was going to receive the inheritance he had been harassing his mother about for years. He received about 580 pounds, a considerable inheritance then. Also, coincidentally, a close friend and political ally, Wilhelm Wolff died and left Marx over 700 pounds. With these sudden bailouts, they paid off their debts and moved into a much more luxurious house, where the Marx family carried on with their profligate ways, but put off financial difficulties for a while.

But then Marx began to have physical problems that would plague him the rest of his life—huge carbuncles on his back, thighs, buttocks, and genitals. They were fist-sized and extremely painful. It was an autoimmune disorder that is difficult to treat even today. In Marx's time, it was impossible. Marx became so frustrated that at one point he took a razor and cut through one of the growths himself. It was a wonder he didn't die from an infection.

At the same time, Jenny contracted smallpox, from which she survived, but it left hideous scars.

Physical problems, personal rivalries, financial problems, fractural quarrels, and a disturbing tide of nationalism and growing global warfare all hindered Marx's ultimate goals.

Then, in 1871 came the Franco-Prussian War, and the Paris Commune, and Marx's optimism resumed. Massive political activity was breaking out everywhere: in the United Kingdom, anti-British activity was rising in Ireland, a new government came to power in Romania, a revolution in Spain, uprisings in southern Italy and violent strikes and demonstrations in the United States. All these activities seemed to be creating a perfect storm for the communist cause.

Also, in 1870 Engels sold his interest in his legal firm and obtained a solid financial foundation that allowed him to support Marx and his family for the rest of his life. He gave Marx an annual income of 350 pounds. This would not end Marx's spendthrift ways, but at least now he had a steady income to keep creditors at bay.

Marx believed in a decentralization and direct democracy. Elected officials would run local communes. Elected officials would be bound by their voters' will and subject to recall if they didn't abide by this. Separation of church and state would be a feature of the new communist state, as well as a secular public education. One can't help but wonder if Karl Marx had studied the writings of Thomas Jefferson.

A huge disappointment and horror for Marx would be the failure of the Paris Commune, to which the government responded by murdering 30,000 people. His association with the Parisian insurgents came to an end. Marx's optimism was wearing thin, and his miserable physical disabilities weren't helping matters.

His glorious vision of communist revolution was growing dimmer.

CHAPTER 5

Marx's writings afterwards became difficult to interpret, as they were fragmentary: pieces of journalism and correspondence. He never produced another definitive theoretical work. He left scores of incomplete manuscripts, including the third volume of *Capital*. He intended in Volume III to discuss banking and credit, which is indispensible to what is happening today, and what many critics of Marx don't understand, even ostensibly well known economists such as Paul Krugman. Marx never got to his deeper analysis of what he called exchange values in forms of capitol. So many think Volume I, the production of value, and the related concept of the Falling Rate of Profit tendency, is Marx's final word on explaining capitalist instability.

Marx repeatedly turned to Darwin to confirm his belief in the evolution of nature into a stable society, endorsing Darwin's theories as positive for human nature. The positivist side of Darwinism undermined the more negative Hegelian ideas. The sad irony in Darwinian theory is that society's evolution manifested itself in the capitalists' survival of the fittest. Laissez-faire capitalism equaled dog eat dog, resulting in the world we currently inhabit, on the verge of ecological and economic ruin. Marx's positivist belief in Darwinian Theory of Natural Selection and the idea of progress ultimately did nothing to improve humanity's lot—in fact the opposite, which in hindsight seems more like devolution.

After Marx died, racism and nationalism began to rear their ugly heads. In Europe began a struggle between what was considered the inferior Slavic and the superior German race. Added to these ideas was that Jews could not be equal citizens. An idea surfaced that Jews should have their own segregated state, and thus emerged the ideas of Zionism, and their own ideas of nationalism.

Marx was well aware of these theories of Aryan superiority and certainly was not in favor of them. He was in favor of the emancipation of Negroes in America. However, like most Europeans of mid-nineteenth century Europe, he viewed Jews in strictly religious and cultural terms, and this was evident in his correspondence, oftentimes using racial language to characterize Jews, showing innate racial prejudice.

In *Capital*, Marx explains that as soon as the exchange of goods such as bartering turned into an exchange of money, trading goods became a means of increasing one's store of money, rather than exchanging one good or service for another. The commodity used to increase this store of money became human labor. For capitalism to succeed, the employer had to make more money than what he had to pay his employees. Adam Smith proposed that the harder a worker worked, the more productive the business would become, and the employer would reward this hard work by increasing the worker's wages. Marx said that human greed would cause the employer to simply pocket the increased profits and exploit the labor as much as they could get away with in order to get even more profits. This would eventually result in a complex class society, Marx opined, containing all the elements toward self-destruction, with the worker unable to control the products of their own labor.

Henry Ford reasoned that he needed to pay his workers at least enough so they could afford to buy the cars they were manufacturing. The Dodge brothers sued, citing that the stockholders held precedence over the welfare of the workers. The Dodge brothers won, and classic capitalist philosophy emerged among the employer class that it was of benefit to them that workers should not be able to afford to buy the vehicles that they build, and workers in the field should not be able to afford to buy the food they picked, et cetera, in essence having a master and serf society in which the serfs are dependent on the master. Tolstoy had his own ideas on this. Much to his wife Sofia's dismay, Tolstoy tried to give land to his serfs. They responded with bewilderment, not knowing what to do with it, having been accustomed to generations of serfdom. Tolstoy was good to his serfs, but not all masters were, similar to slavery in the United States.

Surplus value is the hidden form of profit. Supply and demand was a semblance, rather than the value determined by labor time. Constant and variable labor determined the rate of profit.

Money resulted at the end of the chain of transactions. The use of money to increase value turned money into capital. It was no longer being used to purchase a commodity. It came to an end: profit. This was achieved by cheating the workers: paying them less than the value of their labor.

Driven by competition in the market, in order for the capitalist to increase or at least maintain their level of profits, they had to implement tools such as increasing the workday, lowering wages, creating working conditions that would not dip into expenditures, so on. This extension of absolute surplus value produced a greater proportion of labor time for producing more profit for the employer and a lesser proportion to producing goods, than when sold, would pay their wages. Thus, Marx deduced a dismal portrait of misery and exploitation of labor, even using children, for as many hours as feasible, day and night. Capitalism was all about producing more and producing more productively. The worker must be given just the bare amount of time off and enough food to keep producing at an accelerating rate.

And then, with the advent of the Industrial Age, as production became more mechanized, capitalist demand for labor decreased, driving down wages even more, creating a growing number of workers competing for these lousy jobs, an "industrial reserve army." Immigration and population increase was encouraged with increased industrialization, which creates an overpopulation of the working class.

Marx had oodles of evidence to display his theory. Misery and poverty were omnipresent. Undernourished poor people everywhere populated the streets and poor houses. The lives of these people were worse than conditions in jail or prison.

When Dostoyevsky's *The House of the Dead* became popular in Russia, with its beastly descriptions of prison life, citizens actually began to commit crimes in order to get into these prisons, reasoning that there at least they would be fed, which was more than what they were getting as free persons. People were essentially like animals, spending their lives scrounging for food and some semblance of comfort.

These laws of scientific evolution of capital would accumulate into fewer and fewer hands as the financial demands of the increasing organic composite of capital drove smaller firms out of business. Conglomerations and mergers would occur. Production would be increasingly centralized and mechanized, designed for more efficiency. Productivity would grow at the same time as unemployment increased, eventually globally. And then ultimately, the workers would revolt and an inevitable socialist utopia would emerge. This was Marx's dream.

In *Capital*, he even used mathematical formulas to prove his positivism, algebra and calculus. Marx was not creating new ideas, only elaborating on old ones, ones even described decades earlier in writings by Adam Smith, Thomas Malthus, and John Stuart Mill. Marx's consequences of capitalist society are as real today as they were then. What hasn't happened, of course, is Marx's positivist utopian vision—at least not yet—and as the climate scientists are telling us, it's probably too late.

CHAPTER 6

Few feminists have embraced Marx's ideas. While endorsing women's political participation in the political process, he maintained typical Nineteenth Century views about women. While ostensibly supporting the suffragist movement, his writings show an astonishing contempt for women in general. However, compared to most of his contemporaries, he comes across as enlightened. One can consider the giant mind of Thomas Jefferson and his biased attitudes toward women, African and Native Americans as one example—which from today's perspective seems far from progressive.

And despite his philosophical beliefs, Marx worked to present to the world a family of bourgeois respectability. The great enemy of the bourgeoisie strove to be middle class in his home life, not at all like the proletariat he championed. Critics of course see this as ammunition for hypocrisy. Marx was a product of his upbringing, as much as Jews and Catholics who adopt the traditions of their upbringing when they may not even believe in God. He was a Nineteenth-Century, Anglo-German bourgeois, and not much could change that. He endorsed its culture, struggled to maintain it, and modified it fit his circumstances, which for most of the time meant being mired in debt. Marx had none of the commodities of the bourgeoisie: property, a good income, or security.

This absence continually tore at his conscience throughout his life. Without the generosity of Engels, he would have been in the poor house with the rest of that class he spent his life defending.

Marx's mother maintained a fierce hold on the family assets until her death, infuriating Marx. This only served to emphasize his feelings of failure and the inability to fend for his family as its patriarchal head. He would lie awake at night agonizing over financial worries. While creditors were hounding him, he struggled to maintain appearances. Too ashamed to go to the pawnbrokers himself, he sent Jenny or his housekeeper. Marx ignored all financial dealings in the household, leaving this abysmal task to Jenny, who was no better than her husband at budgeting.

His inability to provide for a dowry for his daughters was a further personal disgrace, displaying additional failure to maintain a bourgeois image. Defenders of Marx would say he was blithe about financial matters as a rejection of bourgeois attitudes toward money, but the truth is that Marx carried deeply hidden guilt and shame about his chronic financial failure. And beside the money he received from Engel's, Marx's income from his journalism wasn't much, despite its widely read popularity.

Marx was open about his Jewish descent, and even expressed pride in it. His deleterious comments about Jews were usually in reference to specific persons, like Lassalle, referencing Lassalle's faults in Jewish stereotypes. Simply put, it is a fault of Marx that cannot be defended. And his personal life is evidence of a desire to present himself as anything but Jewish. Irony abounds. He is a chauvinistic, proud, hard-working German with residues of a Jewish background.

Marx spent much of his life in expectation of the revolution that would not happen in his lifetime. He was deeply disappointed that nothing happened with the global recession in 1857. The 1870s saw the re-emergence of large-scale economic crises throughout Europe and North America. There were stock market crashes, severe recessions, high unemployment, and labor unrest. There were rail strikes and rioting in the United States, but still no communist revolution.

The 1880s saw the capitalists moving into Africa for its vast resources, which put imperialism at the center of these analyses of capitalism. And all this is still going on today: imperialism into mineral rich countries while exploiting and enslaving its people, periodic stock market crashes, high unemployment and exploitation of poor people and immigrants. Over one hundred years later, Marx's views of capitalism are intact and his expected revolution still waiting to happen.

Marx expected that in most countries, the revolution would have to occur through violent means. But he believed that in some nations, such as the United Kingdom, the United States, and the Netherlands—these countries would allow it to happen democratically. In this respect perhaps, Marx was naïve. As we have seen in the United States over and over, the democratic process is pretense, both restricted and repressed.

In Russia, he endorsed the terrorists who had begun a campaign of killing high government officials, striking down police and provincial governments with bullets or explosives. Even so-called pacifist contemporaries such as Victor Hugo and Mark Twain shared with him these pro-terrorists sympathies as necessary.

The idea of a reduced working day and expansion of productivity through automation leaving more time for recreation and creativity was always a philosophy of German *Wissenschaft*. This utopian vision saw a society devoted to artisans and scholarly pursuits. Marx saw this as a positivist scenario, analogous to Darwin's biological evolution, which the progress of stages of modes of production in human history corresponded to the progressive evolutionary development of species in natural history. Marx saw historical development with the glass half full.

Today hundreds of species are going extinct every day. There is ten times as much plastic as life-giving phytoplankton in the oceans.

Of the nation's ancient forests, 95% have been mowed down. The Amazon is losing acres of life sustaining oxygen daily. Migratory songbirds and Monarch butterflies are disappearing. Bee colonies are collapsing. Polar bears and Grizzlies are starving to death, as are many of the world's large fish and whales. Glaciers are melting into the oceans precipitating horrific storms, drought and fire in some areas, flooding in others. There are increased blizzards in the winter and tornadoes in the summer.

Marx's version of a social democracy was stymied at every turn, and an economic system called Capitalism has brought the earth to ruin all in the name of private profits. Clear cuts, decimated oceans, polluted air, nuclear power, and loss of topsoil in corporate agriculture have damaged the earth irreparably. Capitalism has been a metaphorical cancer on the earth and it has metastasized, and it is killing us. We are in a new era whether we want to be or not, and our only choice is to adapt.

And our only scarce hope is to abandon the scourge of capitalism.

The world has no choice but to adopt Marxist principles locally: commune—ism: Building just and sustainable communities through a spirit of camaraderie, peace, and justice. It won't be easy. The human world is a mean environment, and they have guns.

On the other hand, maybe it's time for humans to go. Maybe the

Earth has had it with this predatory species. When we allow nature to work on its own without human intervention, the miracle of nature can do its work. It wouldn't be the first time the earth had a mass extinction.

Humans used to work that way before capitalism entered the picture. Nature is self-organizing and adapting. When this relationship becomes disrupted by an invasive species, forms become competitive with one another rather than working with nature, take over, such as invasive English ivy that climb up native trees for sustenance but smother them. Capitalism is smothering the Earth.

With proper care and respect, Earth provides all we need to survive comfortably. Devastating productive lands and polluting the environment for quick profits have brought us to the biggest crisis humanity has ever faced, larger than the Black Plague of the Middle Ages, larger than the Spanish flu, larger than the Nazi threat, larger than anything. We have disrupted the regenerative capacity of Earth's living systems and accelerated climate change on a global scale. Everywhere on earth the climate is changing dramatically. Predatory capitalism has disrupted the normal cycle of nature.

Marx's version of economics could have prevented this disaster. Marx was human, and as such, far from perfect, especially in his personal life. But he had faith in the power and intelligence of humanity. This perhaps was his fatal flaw, to expect his version of economics to evolve in nature. But our only chance now is to abandon what is destroying us.

We have been programmed to believe that money brings happiness. It is true that money can provide us with financial security under a capitalist system, but that does not guarantee personal happiness. In fact, studies have shown that the more money people have the more miserable they are.

Capitalism promises us comfort, pleasure, friends, and freedom. Is Bill Gates free? Are all those gatekeepers he pays roaming his property with their binoculars and weapons helping maintaining his freedom? Would winning Lotto increase your happiness and freedom? I know this to be true: You will gain a lot more friends; lost relatives will appear like maggots. And studies have shown that the majority of Lotto winners end up filing for bankruptcy. They suddenly have all this money and feel entitled to have more stuff: a bigger house, more vehicles, vacation property, a boat, an RV: the ultimate rewards of the American Dream. Lickety-split, they're head over heels in debt again and need to go back to work.

And society has programmed us to be this way, to keep buying more, using up more gewgaws and the latest high tech gadget, throwing it out and buying more. In this society, money is our ruler and despot. The more we have the more we crave.

It causes people who are already rich to engage in shenanigans such as what scammer Bernie Madoff did, which is really no different than what Wall Street investors do every day. Wall Street and the 401Ks we have been forced to engage in for our retirement are nothing more than pyramid schemes. They take our money, build up the stock market based on nothing tangible or constructive, then when it reaches a bubble, rich people walk away with our retirement, and then when they bankrupt their own financial institutions, the taxpayers are there to bail them out.

"...a casino is child's play, compared to the stock exchange." said Karl Marx.

The need for money keeps us working like slaves, competing with others, struggling against impossible odds, backstabbing friends and co-workers, giving sexual favors. And wanting it all is the exact impulse that is exploited by the ruling class, the usurers and investors, the market manipulators, exploiting our needs for their ends.

Ironically, the worst offenders of this mindset are our Puritan Christians, who have completely ignored the fact that Jesus was a homeless panhandler, with nothing in his possession other than a piece of cloth to cover his nakedness and sandals to protect his feet. He and his followers travelled around preaching and depending on the kindness and hospitality of others. The Puritans turned this on its head, deciding that worldly success was spiritual success, which is exactly the opposite of what Jesus preached—at least according to what I've read about his life. They completely ignore what Jesus said about it being easier for a camel to pass through the eye of the needle than a rich person to get into heaven and to the rich person who asked how he was to get into heaven, which was to give his riches to the poor and follow Jesus.

Learning to live with less gives one a greater sense of security than constantly trying to figure out how to make more money. When you are free of wanting unnecessary stuff you are free of struggling for it.

Also, the less you find you need the less you need to work. Putting less priority in making money and more priority in living life to the fullest will give you a sense of freedom and happiness.

And that in turns creates less need for more space. You will find you don't need that 2500-square foot house with its five bedrooms. The more stuff you accumulate is only more stuff to eventually throw out. The less stuff you need, the less money you try to invest and oftentimes go bankrupt doing so, with more money going into savings, even if your savings is in a shoe box. Less money into financial investments means less money for the banksters, who are only using you to make more money for themselves. Local banks used to be there for the welfare of the community, as in *It's a Wonderful Life*. Then they went global and became predatory. You can't depend on a for profit private bank.

Needing less money also creates more time for leisure, creativity, and philosophical musings—the latter of which terrifies the ruling class. They worry when people start thinking. That's what happened in the sixties when the baby boomers had more time on their hands due to the results of FDR's New Deal, started protesting the established order, and the established order responded by co-opting The Movement, by putting their efforts into destroying radical groups and organized labor and making it harder for kids to go to college. Education and knowledge scares the hell out of the ruling class. And they succeeded. Today the masses watch Fox News and take it as gospel. They idolize buffoons like Donald Trump. By the time Reagan was elected, any semblance of the sixties consciousness had been eradicated. Think only of yourself and this will supposedly "trickle down" onto society, which the Reagan administration also adopted as an economic philosophy: laissez-faire capitalism. And we have been living with supply side economics ever since, whether it is under a Republican or Democrat. Barack Obama learned everything he knows about economics from the neoliberal philosophy taught at the Chicago School of Economics under Milton Friedman.

The selfishness and narcissistic psychosis that is inherent in the capitalist system has resulted in the world we inhabit today, one on the brink of destruction. We have no choice but to adapt. It is too late for the millions of plant and animal species which have gone extinct. It is too late for the billions who have died from abject poverty and disease. But through the ideals that are at the core of our hearts and spirit, we can perhaps survive and avoid complete human extinction, and with it preserve the marvelous ideas that came out of human intelligence: culture, art, science, and architecture.

Marx's vision of a socialist utopia failed to materialize, and today multinationals create destruction, murder, pollution and chaos around the world in search of the cheapest, most exploitive workforce they can find, and the politicians enable them with one trade pact after another.

PART THREE

DARWIN AND EXTINCTION

CHAPTER 1

According to current scientific thought, there have been five mass extinctions in Earth's history. And according to climatologists, we are now in the sixth, and it's human-caused, a result of the human greed that inspired free enterprise. That's it in a nutshell.

The human species began about 200,000 years ago. They were a particularly fragile species physically: weak and slow, but they had one advantage over most other species: an evolved brain. It is now believed that humans migrated out of Africa to gradually spread across the globe. Over eons of time, during gradual climate changes, continents connected and disconnected and humans were able to slowly adapt to their environment through evolution. They developed tools and other advanced ideas for hunting and very likely hunted the giant mastodon into extinction. They used these and other animals for food and clothing. They found that fire cooked meat and made it more palatable. Fire also created warmth and scared off other predatory animals. They were innovative and found that migration provided means for more food and better climate. It is now believed that they mated and warred with Neanderthals, eventually killing that species off, and evolving from it.

Over tens of thousands of years, humans grew in population, went from hunter/gatherers to farmers and craftsmen. Places such as Iceland, Ireland, and New Zealand were deforested for fuel and homes. In warm climates, however, such as Africa and Australia, the native population didn't need to keep warm by burning wood, and had everything they needed in their environment to sustain themselves.

About 300 years ago it was discovered that coal and oil was useful as fuel, and then people began selling it as a commodity. At the beginning of the twentieth century, diesel fuel was invented by Rudolph Diesel. At first meant to be created from vegetable oils, it was quickly redesigned to be produced by the fractional distillation of crude oil, resulting in a more toxic emission. The release of these carbons into the atmosphere contributed to climate change.

The first recorded mention of climate change came in the early nineteenth century. Joseph Fournier in 1824 wrote about a process by which radioactive energy leaving the planet in the burning of wood, oil, and coal is absorbed into the atmosphere and re-radiated in all directions, including back to earth, creating a "greenhouse" effect, and an artificial warming of the planet.

CHAPTER 2

The first paleontologists suggested that the earth had previously experienced mass extinctions. A French scientist by the name of Georges Cuvier studied the extinction of mastodons. Thomas Jefferson was fascinated with Cuvier's work, which was widely popular.

Curiously, Cuvier didn't believe in evolution. Evolution was first proposed not by Charles Darwin, but by a French naturalist by the name of Jean-Baptiste Lamarack. Lamarack proposed that animals adapted to their environment by physically adopting new habits and physically modified to this adaptation through reproduction. Cuvier declared Lamarack's ideas absurd, pointing out that cats after thousands of years were still cats. Lamarack replied that these particular cats to which he was referring had not been required to adapt, and in fact cats over much longer periods *had* adapted, and evolved into leopards, lions, house cats, etc. Without evolution, Lamarack posited, none of the species on Earth would exist. The thousands of years Cuvier referred to was "an infinitely small duration in the life of the Earth." Lamarck also believed that all dog species had evolved from wolves.

Naïve about evolution, it was Cuvier, nevertheless, who first speculated that a huge global catastrophe resulted in a mass extinction. However, he was incorrect in associating the disappearance of the dinosaurs with the mastodon. This huge, powerful animal was wiped out by the lowly human, the first indication that humans were too smart and greedy for their own good.

Darwin's study of coral reefs was his first hint in discovering the interplay between biology and geology. He discovered that corals maintained their positive relation to water by slowing growing upwards. As the lands subsided, the coral formed a barrier reef. If the land sank away entirely, the reef would form an etoll. This revelation was astounding to him, and when he proposed his ideas to his colleague Charles Lyell, Lyell realized that what Darwin had discovered was revolutionary. This eventually became Darwin's "Theory of Natural Selection", or Evolution, which today is no long regarded as a theory by scientists, but a biological, irrefutable fact. He established that not only water and land adapted to gradual change, but plants and animals, and that humans came into being through a reproductive transformation over generations. Natural Selection put to question the idea of a Supreme Being that created the universe and everything in it. Darwin wrote: "The appearance of new forms and disappearance of old forms were bound together…in a struggle for existence," the survival of the fittest. "…each new species, is produced and maintained by having advantages over those with whom it comes into competition: and the consequential extinction of less favored forms almost inevitably follows."

Darwin, however, rejected Cuvier's thesis of mass extinction, believing that world-altering catastrophes could be avoided by simply by Natural Selection, which he believed was a gradual phenomenon, not a sudden one.

The Great Auk (pinguinus impennis) was a large bulky bird about four feet tall with small wings and though much like penguins, couldn't fly, and was very slow on land, which made them vulnerable to prey. They laid only one egg a year, which also was considered a tasty morsel. It lived in the northern hemisphere and at one time its population was over a million. They were good swimmers and spent much of their time in the sea, coming to land in May and June to breed. And this was when their greatest prey lay in wait. Over just several decades, the Great Auk was rendered extinct. In addition to food, they used the feathers. By 1830, when John James Audubon went looking for a Great Auk to paint, he couldn't find any. The last people to reportedly see any Great Auks were reportedly a dozen Icelanders who made a trip to an island called Geirfuglasker. The birds tried to run from their predators, but as usual, they were too slow. It was likely here that the last of the Great Auks were slaughtered. No species that has gone extinct has ever returned.

This indicates what a crapshoot life forms are.

Darwin was aware of the human involvement in extinction. He witnessed such action first hand at the Galapagos Islands, where there were some of the most diverse species on Earth. "Humans could survive quite well on the Galapagos." The islands were often visited by whaling ships, which collected tortoises for sustenance. Darwin could see that these tortoises' days were numbered; they were wiped out in about ten years. He wrote in *The Origin of Species* : "We know this has been the progress of events with those animals which have been exterminated, either locally or wholly, through mass agency."

Amazingly, however, this did not alarm Darwin, who simply considered the extinction of species as evidence of his theory of natural selection through superior competition. The Earth was awash in species, after all.

And his lack of worry may have had credence if not for the following two phenomenon: free enterprise and overpopulation.

CHAPTER 3

Scientists believe that the asteroid that ended the Cretaceous period was probably the greatest disaster for species ever on Earth, the evidence of which suggested that extinction was not always, as Darwin had said, a slow and gradual process, but an almost immediate one. It is estimated the asteroid was about six miles wide, and its impact created the released energy of more that a million of the most powerful H-bombs every tested. Debris, including iridium from the pulverized asteroid, spread across the globe. Day turned to night and temperatures plunged. A mass extinction followed. This was recorded in a publication in 1980 by Walter Alvarez called, "Extraterrestrial Cause for the Cretaceous Tertiary Extinction." Astrophysicist Carl Sagan called this a "nuclear winter" which became a term used as a result of a nuclear war, one of the two phenomena that are the greatest threat to the survival of species on the Earth, the other of course being global warming. His theory was debated by scientists and now is generally considered true.

During the late Cretaceous period the world was very warm; lush forests grew in the Arctic. The world's land continents were much narrower, New York under water. Anthropologists have found fossilized sharks and ammonite fossils far inland from today's seas.

When the asteroid hit, the world's forests were decimated and it is estimated that every animal larger than a small cat was wiped out, the most famous victim being the dinosaurs, or at least the non-avian dinosaurs. About two-thirds of all bird species were gone, four-fifths of all lizards and snakes, and two-thirds of the world's mammals. There were also heavy casualties in the seas. All living things today are descended from the survivors of that impact. Such is the power of evolution.

Darwin thought that each species that had gone extinct did so in a "struggle for life" as a "less improved form." He believed there was a uniformitarian rule to extinction and that this happened very slowly. The discovery of the end of the Cretaceous era caused scientists to realize that that it can happen suddenly and chaotically through catastrophe.

We are witnessing today this latter extinction. There is another catastrophe ongoing right now. Scientists know that changing weather patterns alter life and derail evolution. The difference between today and what happened when the asteroid hit is that it is the result of human actions, the release of too much CO_2 into the atmosphere. A pattern of quick extinction is such that it is estimated that 200 species on Earth are going extinct every day.

The end of the Permian period also seems to have been caused by change in climate. At the time of this extinction, 252 million years ago, there was a massive release of carbon into the air, and scientists still are puzzled where the carbon came from. Temperatures soared, and the seas warmed by as much as 18 degrees. The chemistry of the ocean went haywire. Organism suffocated. Reefs collapsed. But get this: according to scientists, the episode lasted *100,000 years* or more. By the time it was over, something like 90% of all species on Earth were extinct. Science writers describe the end-Permian period world as a truly grotesque place, like out of a science fiction film—with slurry, purple seas releasing poisonous bubbles that rose to a pale green, noxious sky.

CHAPTER 4

Paul Crutzen, a Dutch chemist, was one of the first scientists to discover the effects of ozone-depleting chemicals into the atmosphere. Had they not discontinued the use of these commercial compounds, the ozone "hole" that opens up every spring over Antarctica would have eventually encircled the earth. The value of this discovery is immeasurable and indicative of what we can do as humans if we have a mind to.

Crutzen declared the following changes that have occurred due to climate change:

Human activity has transferred between a third and a half of the land surface on Earth.

1. Many of the world's major rivers have been damaged or diverted.

2. Fertilized plants produce more nitrogen than all other terrestrial ecosystems.

3. Fishing has removed more than a third of the primary populations of the ocean's coastal waters.

4. Humans use more than half of the world's available water run-off.

5. According to Crutzen, humans have altered the composition of the atmosphere.

Due to the combustion of fossil fuels combined with deforestation, the amount of CO_2 into the atmosphere has risen by 40% over the last two centuries. The release of methane, including from farm animals, an even more potent greenhouse gas, has more than doubled. "Because of these anthropogenic emissions," Crutzen says, the global climate is "likely to depart significantly from natural behavior for many millenniums to come."

During the last couple centuries, since the start of the industrial revolution, humans have burned enough fossil fuels—coal, oil, and natural gas—to put some 365 billion metric tons of carbon into the atmosphere. Deforestation has contributed another 180 billion tons. Each year, we emit another nine billion tons, an amount that has increased despite our environmental consciousness. As a result, the concentration of carbon dioxide in the atmosphere is higher than at any point in the past million years. It is expected that this will result in a temperature increase between four and seven degrees Fahrenheit by 2050, which will in turn trigger a variety of earth-altering events, the disappearance of most of the world's glaciers, the flooding of coastal cities and the complete melting of the Arctic ice cap.

What's even worse is the effect of carbon dioxide gas in our oceans, disrupting the delicate balance of oxygen and carbon dioxide. Today the oceans are 30% more acidic than they were in 1800. That, along with overfishing, has resulted in many of the species in the ocean already becoming extinct, and all the oceans large fish are in danger of extinction. Most of the oceans' species are expected to perish. There will be more toxic algae. It will deleteriously affect photosynthesis. The oceans have absorbed one-third of the CO_2 humans have put into the air.

The Great Barrier Reef is the world's largest reef system, composed of 2,900 independent reefs and 900 islands located in the Coral Sea off the coast of Queensland, Australia. The reef structure is composed of tiny organisms called coral polyps. Much of the ocean species depend on the corals for their survival, either directly for food, or indirectly, from predators that prey on these species such as seabirds and turtles. Because of climate change, that reef is dying, according to Ove Hoegh-Guldbgerg, a scientific researcher in the Great Barrier Reef, who says that if this happens it would have immeasurably disastrous effects on the world's ecosystem. He estimates at current rates, the reef would be destroyed by 2050.

Climate change, overfishing, and pollution are the primary threats to the reef system. The Great Barrier Reef Marine Park Authority considers climate change its biggest threat.

With that and ongoing devastating droughts, Australia is a virtual petri dish for human-caused climate change, yet despite that current

Prime Minister Tony Abbot has succeeded in a campaign pledge to eliminate environmental consciousness to match his personal free-market mindset.

Overfishing too has disrupted food chains vital to reef life. Included in the overfishing is the collateral damage of catching unintentional species such as dolphins and turtles, as well as habitat destruction from trawling and use of nets.

It is believed that Aboriginal Australia had been part of the diversity chain for 40,000 years before the White Man came. They had evolved to a species (similar to other indigenous humans) with a seemingly magical spiritual consciousness that has now been virtually abolished by expansionism from Europe.

A program is in place to save the Coral Reef, but it is questionable whether or not it has already passed the tipping point of survival, according to scientists, because of a saturation rate that has prevented calcification, essential for survival. "A few decades ago I, myself, would have thought it ridiculous to imagine that reefs might have limited lifespans," J.E.N. Veron, former chief scientists of the Australian Institute of Marine Science, has written: "Yet here I am utterly convinced that they will not be here for our children's children to enjoy."

CHAPTER 5

Today perennial ice caps in the poles are half of what they were just thirty years ago, and in thirty years, they may be gone altogether. Besides the obvious impact on rising coastline and species such as polar bears and penguins, this will also impact the tropics, where most of the world's species exist.

Traveling south from the North Pole, there are species that depend on the glaciers, most notably trees in Canada, such as black spruce, white birch, and balsam fir—as well as about 17 other tree species. This diversity increases in the United States, where there are hundreds of tree species dependent upon the diversity of nature. Across the equator into Latin America, this diversity of trees rises to a staggering level. Thousands of tree species depend upon a corridor of life that begins in the North Pole.

And then of course other species depend on the trees for survival. Without trees, for example, there would be no oxygen, unless it is true what Ronald Reagan said, "trees pollute." But of course they don't, we all learned in grade school that trees breathe carbon dioxide and emit oxygen and we breathe oxygen and emit carbon dioxide. And thus a perfect balance in life evolved for all species.

It is believed that the Amazon is millions of years old. As the rainforests evolved, different species evolved from it. In the Americas there are individual trees that are thousands of years old, alive when Jesus was born, such as Giant Sequoia and Patagonian Cypress.

Given a chance, these trees would conceivably have continued to evolve. But unfortunately, they encountered a major hindrance in a human inspired system of monetary exchange, which included clear-cutting of trees for profit. Today, acres of rainforest trees are being cleared daily for the cause of free enterprise, mostly to make way for cattle for McDonald's burgers, and palm and soy farms, which are ironically mostly used to create biodiesel fuel.

It is believed by scientists that global warming today is increasing at a pace ten times faster than after the last Ice Age. In order to keep up with the pace of the last warming period, organisms have to adapt.

We are running out of time.

In ecological science there is a universally accepted rule called "species-area relationship", a rule that says the greater area of land there is the greater number of species that can exist on that land. This rule has been disrupted by human development, which has spread into habitat once occupied by other species. Thus, people are alarmed when bears are rummaging through their garbage.

Development, agriculture, and industry have converted forests into farmland, industries, shopping malls and housing developments. In order to survive, other species either have to adapt to their new environment, or migrate. Failing to do so, species go extinct—such as wolves, which do only what predatory animals do, prey on more vulnerable animals for sustenance in this balance of nature, and ranchers are given legal rights to shoot them, disrupting that balance, and rendering another beautiful animal nearly extinct.

In the abstract, one might conclude that there is no reason for certain species not to adapt to a warmer planet and continue to evolve. In the short term, however, the human species is facing obvious challenges. In the long term, if they are to survive they have to change their metabolism in order to adapt, according to Chris Thomas, a biologist at the University of York.

Scientists say that some species are going to benefit from global warming, one of which are rats. Rats have managed to migrate to just about everywhere on Earth today, and some scientists believe that they will take over the earth. In evolutionary terms, they say, rats are most prepared to adapt to migration, one of the most invasive species there are. Europeans came to America with Norway rats on their ships. "Norway" rats probably originally came from China, and in America began ravaging the bird and reptile populations. Rats of the future are expected to evolve to the size of elephants.

Scientists refer to extinction as "biotic attrition", a nice scientific euphemism, which means we humans are most likely, screwed.

Darwin was greatly puzzled by why there was such an incredible diversity of species on the Galapagos Islands, not that they existed, but where they came from. Five hundred miles of water separated the islands from the coast of South America. He finally concluded that they had to have somehow migrated by sea or air. He discovered that a seal could travel more than a 1000 miles in six weeks, a duck six or seven hundred miles.

After Darwin's death, Darwin's ideas about "geographical distribution" advanced to include the changing geography of the earth, the connecting and displacement of continents. Since reptiles and other species were discovered in places where they had no business, it was assumed that the Pacific and Atlantic oceans once had vast land bridges between continents, constantly shifting. It is hypothesized that all present day continents had been "supercontinent" resulting in "continental drifts". The discovery of plate tectonics pretty much confirmed this theory.

Today's "geographical distribution" has come in the migration of species to other parts of the earth through global trade. The result has been that in some parts of the world, non-native species are smothering out native ones. Probably the most compelling example of this is in New

Zealand, which along with Australia and accompanying islands once had some of the most diverse and unique species on the planet. Because of clear-cutting and immigration of species such as rabbits, sheep and rats, nearly all the original species in New Zealand have gone extinct.

Due to unsuitable climates, most migratory species don't survive. But in many cases, not only do they survive; they take over, each generation becoming stronger and more adaptable, such as pythons in the Everglades in Florida, English Ivy and Himalayan blackberry in the northwest United States. A certain beetle that originated from Japan called papilla japonica has infected North America and is destroying forests.

The American chestnut was once a dominant deciduous tree in eastern forests of the U.S. In Connecticut, making up half of the standing timber. Around the turn of the century, a certain fungus was introduced called cryphonectria parasitica, also from Japan it is believed, resulting in chestnut blight. Asian chestnut had evolved to resist this fungus, but the American chestnut had no resistance to it—very similar to how smallpox practically wiped out indigenous Americans. By 1950, some four billion trees were wiped out. Practically every species that depended on the chestnut trees also were wiped out, such as several species of moths.

On the predatory scale, one of the species that is on top is the elephant. Other animals because of the elephants' immense size and strength do not hunt it. Elephants are also very intelligent and social animals that have shown to experience intense grief with deaths in the family. Humans, who killed elephants for their ivory tusks, disrupted this advantage of size. And thus, because of its commercial value, elephants are now nearly extinct, a result of commercial greed.

The extraction of forests for commercial use and burning of land to make way for agriculture has had similar results. As such, humans have been too smart for their own good, resulting in global warming and the possibility of their own extinction. Despite being quite aware that we are killing ourselves, commercial extractions of resources such as oil, coal and natural gas carry on unremittingly. The oil and gas companies are licking their chops in anticipation of the melting ice caps so they can drill for more oil, their overwhelming greed displacing common sense.

All the great apes today are facing extinction. The reasons for this are poaching, disease, and habitat loss. The multiplication of humans and its regional conflicts have also been a major cause. Despite efforts to save the great apes, elephants, hippos, and other large animals through conservation efforts it is highly likely these wonderful top-of-the food chain beasts will soon no longer be with us. In addition, habitat is disappearing because of logging, legal and illegal.

The more forward thinking and altruistic of us humans have been unable to complete with the shortsighted greed of monetary gain. We have not learned how to share the earth's bounty; we have instead exploited it. And scientists, such as biology scientists, who should be studying that which their degree enables them, are hired by corporations, who offer them salaries of which it is difficult to resist, because they like all of us, have to survive in a capitalist world.

The current extinction is not the result of glaciation as at the end of the Ordovician era, global warming at the end of the Permian, or the impact of a huge asteroid at the abrupt end of the Cretaceous. The current extinction is caused by the unbridled greed of human beings that developed a convenient monetary system. Our lives are perhaps more convenient with cars, airplanes, refrigerators, air conditioners and smart phones. But because of clear-cutting vital forests, wiping out beautiful creatures, acidifying the oceans, putting CO_2 into the atmosphere—all for private profits—we have put most species, including our own, on the precipice of disaster.

The Amazon is considered the lungs of *Gaia*.

The Arctic poles are considered its cooling system.

A greed inspired economic system is destroying them both.

PART FOUR

WHAT WE CAN DO

CHAPTER 1

Most likely, we can do nothing to stop this ecological holocaust. It's too late. Global warming, according to many climatologists, is past the tipping point in which to reverse the snowball effect of global warming. Many scientists have thrown up their hands in surrender. But we have to try, don't we? There is nothing else we *can* do.

The bad news is that the ones in charge are the transnational mega-corporations that enforce the free-market economy in the formulas of coal mining, oil production, nuclear, logging, planned obsolescence products to ensure the free-market cycle, a corporate-owned media that maintains societal ignorance and pushes free-market propaganda and continues to mass produce gas combustion engines. The good news is that the world population is becoming more and more aware of this oppressive supremacy and is starting to do something about it. They are beginning to understand the parasitic nature of free-market capitalism. Most young people especially are quite aware that if something isn't done fast, we are in deep trouble. The change that is necessary, an economy that sustains nature rather than exploits it is ongoing: a free internet, the slow food movement, bicycling and rail transportation solar, more wind farms, more tree planting and refusing, reducing, reusing and recycling. All these activities are thriving, and they must continue to grow fast—fast enough to overwhelm capitalism.

And reducing the population is essential, probably the most important thing we can do, because if we don't do it voluntarily, nature will do it for us. China and India with over a third of the world's seven billion people have been attempting desperately to join the fossil-fuel based, consume-and-throw-away capitalist economy that in just a few hundred years has brought us to the ecological holocaust we face today. Sure, they are building solar panels, but they also have the most polluted cities in the world.

The capitalist mindset of the past three hundred years has resulted in a multiplication of the human species that is unprecedented in Earth's history. Uncontrolled growth in bodies in unison with economic growth has brought us to this brink. And a cancerous neoliberal policy of spreading that growth worldwide with clearing land, building power plants, fossil fuel-driven vehicles, polluting airplanes, air-conditioning, refrigeration, and agri-business has all contributed to it. And nature has responded with viruses, allergens, cancers and other diseases that have been spread through the modern day transportation system. The pace of economic history mingling with the economic demands has collided with the earth's natural limits. The intellectual community is quite aware of this crisis, but they are stuck in this paradigm that assumes somehow that capitalism is the answer rather than the cause. Their shortsighted efforts to maximize profits are simply ecologically unsustainable. A dramatic transference from this economic paradigm to one that works in unison with nature rather than exploitive of it is essential.

It isn't going to be easy or fun, but it can be challenging and rewarding. The major obstacle we face is the corporate/political leaders who rule, and they are currently responding to our demand for change violently. We see it everywhere. They are not going to accept these necessary changes voluntarily. They are too ensconced in their capitalist/fascist paradigm of market signals.

To break through this paradigm is essential if civilization and most of the species on the planet are to survive. We can and must build an economy that works with nature, not against it.

The world today is ruled by a system of commerce in which a handful of elites live in absurd opulence while most of the billions in the world live in abject poverty, too poverty-stricken to concern themselves about global warming; they have enough worries keeping their family fed and a roof over their heads. But as we have seen, many are willing to join extremist groups and kill people. They are bitter. And they know from where their bitterness stems: the United States political elite, which has spread their philosophy of *laissez-faire* capitalism worldwide.

As the rich got richer, the poor got poorer. To add insult to injury, Monsanto has infected world farms with genetically altered seeds, ruining the land and ruining farmers' livelihoods. This psychosis for ever increasing wealth beyond most of our wildest dreams is pursued without moral restraint or public conscience. They are so insulated from the suffering of the poor that they literally cannot see what they have done to people, and to the planet. Like any addiction, money is pursued obsessively with total disregard for what is right and logical. And as a result, the impoverished people of Asia, the Mideast, and Latin America are thrust into rebellion, and our leaders in Washington D.C. scratch their butts and brainstorm dully on how to quell them with American military might.

And we in the major industrial "middle-class" need to take to the streets as well. We did so in Seattle in 1999, and we did in the Occupy Movement. The elite political power quelled both movements temporarily, but like a fire that continues to fester after it's put out, the movement is still festering, still brewing, and it is about to burst out into fire. It is time to get radical. It's going to take more than peaceful protesting. It's going to take some radical monkey wrenching. On a local level it can be eco-movements to prevent overdevelopment. When that which is legal is morally and intellectually bankrupt, it may become necessary to act illegally. Those in power are not going to lay down their arms peacefully and let us have our way without a fight.

During the Occupy Movement in downtown Seattle I talked to some cops who were there doing what they are paid to do. Many of them are on our side. They are struggling too. The economic disparity in wealth has affected them as much as most of us, and they see what's going on. When fascism has taken control of our lives, lawlessness becomes morally defensible.

Rich environmental activists such as Al Gore and Bill McKibben think we can reverse the effects of global warming within the very system that created it. They encourage us to purchase hybrid vehicles and go shopping with cloth shopping bags. That's all fine and good, but guess what? It's too late for just that to save us. It's past the tipping point, and all we can do now is try to live with what we are facing on a dramatically changing planet. More realistic climate scientists such as James Hanson (other than his unrealistic position on nuclear energy) have said that carbon taxes and electric vehicles solve nothing, and individual lifestyle adjustments are a delusional fantasy.

It is imperative that we take down the system of a world controlled by a corporate fascist elite, dismantle Wall Street altogether, and replace the Plutocrats in our three branches of government with those who will represent the earth and its inhabitants rather than the corporatists. Every four years we vote for the "lesser of two evils" for president, the obvious result being we perpetually have a president who is evil. As I write these words it is likely that next evil person to be president of the Unites States is going to be either Hillary Clinton or Jeb Bush, two of the most corporate friendly politicians there are, who will continue the status quo of the free-market ruin of the Earth, maintaining it with the most powerful military in the world. I know voting for whoever is running in the Green party or Libertarian party is a wasted vote, but so is voting for Hillary Clinton. Our votes are meaningless because we don't have a genuine democracy, despite the propaganda to the contrary.

CHAPTER 2

As I said earlier in this book, American democracy ended with the assassination of JFK. Ever since then, our votes, at least on the national scale, have been meaningless. The Kennedys, Martin Luther King, Malcolm X, among others assassinated who were not so well publicized (perhaps even Paul Wellstone) were a hindrance to the industrial/military elite, and so were eliminated without so much forethought as squashing a bug.

After the rebellious and celebratory sixties a mood of cynicism replaced the optimism with a murder in a rock concert in Altamont and a psychotic Charles Manson.

The resignation of Richard Nixon on the eve of being impeached because of the Watergate scandal indicated to the Left that our democratic institutions were still intact. But the celebrations were short-lived, since it led to Ronald Reagan, and this time nothing was done about Arms for Hostages and then Arms for the Contras, two scandals worse than Watergate. Clinton gave us NAFTA and GATT, shipping American jobs overseas so corporations could exploit slave labor, this time by a Democrat of all things, as well as rescinded Glass-Steagall. And then arrived George W. Bush, with his lies about getting us into the war in Iraq and then discovering that the administration not only condoned, but encouraged, torture.

Barack Obama became our first Black president, but it meant nothing for the cause of democracy as he continued to do the duty of the financial power elite. He ignored Bush's criminal offenses as he told us to "look to the future and not dwell on the past." If he hadn't done that, he would have been eliminated. An illegal surveillance was put on Americans more pronounced than any other president in history, including Nixon and George W. Bush. Drone strikes have murdered innocent people, including the elderly, women and children. Our current president is as much war criminal as George W. Bush and Dick Cheney.

Industrial water consumption is drying up water supplies all over the world. The amount of water used to constantly cool nuclear reactors alone is of gargantuan proportions. The same water we have always had on earth is still here, but it is taking new forms in the melting of the ice caps and the toxicity of industrialization. Industrial drilling for water has resulted in major drops in water tables. Small and subsistence farms are quickly losing their necessary water supplies. Massive droughts and flooding throughout the world is further depleting it.

And then there's "fracking", a procedure to extract natural gas deep within the earth involves a procedure officially called "high-volume horizontal hydraulic fracturing." They inject gigantic amounts of water mixed with toxic chemicals and sand at high pressure to build up rock formations and release the gas. *Trillions* of gallons of water have been laced with corrosive salts, carcinogens like benzene and radioactive elements like radium, along with other carcinogens and materials. This procedure fractures the earth surrounding it, like an earthquake. The industry has been lying to us on the safety of this procedure and its toxic effect to the communities close to it.

Wastewater is hauled to sewage plants not prepared to treat it and then discharged into rivers that supply water to communities. This has contaminated the drinking water to those who live close to the fracking. A documentarian, Josh Fox, did a film called "Gasland", in which he interviewed farmers who lived close to the fracking, and people turned on their taps, put a light to the water, and it ignited.

One cause and effect piles onto another. According to scientists, the melting of the ice caps has resulted in methane release, which contributes even more to global warming. The problem is progressive, not problematic or hypothetical. It is real; it is not debatable, as our politicians have pretended it to be. The problem was real before it became evident to us, and the more transparent it is, the harder the corporatists work to dismiss it as a hoax.

Even when someone tries to operate an environmentally sustainable corporation, the company is outcompeted in the laws of supply and demand.

When Monsanto genetically alters a plant they are not doing it to help feed people, they are doing it to make money—and poisoning the people in the process. Not only are they poisoning us, according to a just released thirty-year study of comparing organic food with chemical agriculture, the conclusion is that organic production is far superior to that used with chemicals. As far as production results, the organic outpaces the conventional, even during years of drought. It builds richer soil. It uses half the energy. It produces half the greenhouse gases, and it is actually more profitable. And yet it is too expensive for most Americans to purchase.

Nuclear power utility companies are not providing energy; they are making money. It requires more energy to produce nuclear power than the energy provided, which means it receives government subsidies to maintain its profits. It is also dangerous and toxic, as the latest nuclear disaster in Fukushima, Japan demonstrated. They still haven't a clue what to do with the nuclear waste that has been piling up for the last sixty years, waste that must be sequestered from all living things for tens of thousands of years, which by the way, hasn't been done. Their solution has been to store them in stainless steel lined drums until they come up with a permanent solution. These barrels are leaking, and a solution doesn't exist. The cancer rate of those who live in the vicinity of nuclear power plants has risen exponentially from the release of nuclear waste.

Another convenient use of the waste has been depleted uranium in weaponry released in Afghanistan, Iraq, Bosnia, Kosovo, and elsewhere. DU emits an ionizing radiation responsible for inevitable genetic damage, cancer, and an assortment of lethal kidney/liver diseases, and death.

Despite propaganda that nuclear power is a "green" energy source, actually vast amounts of carbon are emitted in the transportation and enrichment of uranium, and it takes ten to twenty years to build a nuclear plant, dramatically increasing costs that the taxpayer is expected to pay.

In addition to this of course is the potentiality of terrorists obtaining enough fission material to build a "dirty bomb" and the increased expense of guarding these materials, and more burdens on the taxpayer.

Coal and oil when left in the ground actually serve a function to the ecosystem. It is (or was) the Earth's compost system. They sequester the carbon long ago pulled out of the ground by plants. They also absorb other toxins, such as cadmium, mercury and uranium. When oil and coal are pulled out of the ground they stop serving these necessary functions of nature, and when they are released in the air they create more poisons in our atmosphere. The burning of coal has been a plague on the world since the dawn of the Industrial Revolution, causing heart, respiratory, and other diseases, including cancer.

And the Keystone XL pipeline that the Canadian oil industry wants to build from Canada to the Gulf of Mexico to be shipped out on the international market, stems from one of the dirtiest and most polluting gunk of oil there is. It starts with a habitable ecosystem teeming with life and turns into a parched, empty desert where nothing can live, mining a semi-solid goo known as bitumen that is so difficult to extract it up to four times more labor intensive than conventional oil.

Add to this the disruption to the environment while the pipeline is being built, and once built and running, the chances of an oil spill are not if, but when. After years of waffling on the subject, Obama has finally leaned toward not building it, probably because of all the protesting that has been done by the environmental community. The current Republican majority in Congress, however, is determined to allow it to be built, and it will then depend on Obama to veto it. And his history defying the fossil fuel industry is far from laudable.

Capitalist shell games and carbon trading scams allow companies to make even more profits while avoiding genuine accountability and doing nothing to slow global warming. How long do we allow this to continue? One would think that a looming mass extinction would cause them to rethink their goals. But they don't think; they are too ensconced in their psychotic need for more money despite whatever consequences. Like schizoid psychotics, they lack empathy for anything outside their narrow sphere of private profits. All they think about is the bottom line, future consequences be damned. They are extremely powerful, and they are backed by the most powerful military in history. And now a fire has been lit under us, and we are responding. They look out their windows on Wall Street and elsewhere at the protestors and are nonplussed. They genuinely don't get it. "Let them eat the crumbs of the cake we are tossing at them."

Reformers to laissez-faire capitalism are historically referred to as "liberals". These liberals depend on the government to keep a leash on corporate corruption and mismanagement. This was most markedly represented in FDR's New Deal, which implemented reforms during the Great Depression in order to save capitalism from the excesses of itself and probably avoided a revolution like what happened in Russia. This is classic Keynesian liberalism, which has from its inception worked to enable capitalism with regulations and restraints. Thus, we have no genuine Left, because a real Left would reject capitalism outright and replace it with a system that embraces human needs and environmental protection, not private profits. Congress is actually two wings of the same party: the Corporate Party.

Real reformers are sabotaged. Eliot Spitzer, Elizabeth Warren, Van Jones, and others are given lip service by those in power, and then tossed out on their ears. If by some divine intervention, Elizabeth Warren or Bernie Sanders were to be elected president, they would either conform (to which both have displayed ample evidence of doing so), or not be allowed to proceed with their agenda by Congress, impeached, or at the last resort, assassinated. Every attempt to reform capitalism's excesses has been derailed.

It is obvious then that we cannot depend on a system that is beyond redemption. We can't act nice and say pretty please with peanut butter on it.

George Bernard Shaw said: "Revolutions have never lightened the burden of tyranny; they have only shifted the burden to another's shoulders." And history has shown this to be largely true. The revolutions that have been toppling governments in the Mideast will not likely result in a harmonic convergence of utopian splendor; it will more likely result in just more despots. And those despots better represent American interests—or watch out. A true democracy that genuinely represents the welfare of the people (such as nationalization of resources and equitable distribution of wealth) would not be allowed by the United States or Britain. When a democratic Muslim government was formed in Somalia (and doing well by the way), the United States intervened and backed an invasion by the "Christian" government of Ethiopia, and chaos resulted.

How can we blame Somalians when they then join terrorist groups like al Qaeda?

Pleading and begging with corporations to face the reality of global warming will not work because they are too far gone to care. These billionaires care only for their next quarterly report, consequences be damned. Typical liberal reformers don't seem to understand the breadth of that power; they really think they can contain these unbridled psychotics. They keep on electing people like Bill Clinton and Barack Obama expecting them to implement concrete reforms and restraints on this corporate power, and each time they are elected they just keep on representing the interests of the corporatists instead. "Obama is getting bad advice from those who surround him," is a typical liberal copout. Who surrounded him with these people?

Nonviolence is an effective tool when used on a massive scale led by someone of immense charisma. Mohandas Gandhi, JFK and MLK were three who had that charisma, and they got results. And we know what happened to them. These men today would be horrified by what has happened in each of their countries since. Gandhi was elderly, but MLK was only 39, JFK 42. We can't lose sight of the breadth of power that corporations have and resorting to violence may become an inevitable defense mechanism.

Under the global economy of classic capitalism, even so-called Leftist governments, such as Norway, Venezuela, and Bolivia, continue to use oil as an economic resource.

They may use it for social good, but it still contributes to global warming. They do it because they have no choice if they are to provide for their people, under the global tyranny of capitalism.

Recently, David Cameron's Conservative Party maintained a majority of seats in Great Britain. In Canada, Conservative Party member Stephen Harper is Prime Minister. In Australia, it's Tony Abbott, a climate change denier. We might as well have a global grand slam and have Jeb Bush President of the United States in 2016. All these world leaders are calling for austerity, to promote growth in the economy by having the mass of people do less. Cameron, like Margaret Thatcher, has lowered social benefits even more. Like Ronald Reagan, he says, "The State is the problem, not the solution." It has to be shrunk, he says, limiting itself to enforcing rules (i.e., a police state), and letting the markets and the private sector produce wealth.

Economist Paul Krugman says over and over that austerity measures never work, that spending is necessary to stimulate economic growth. This is classic Keynesian philosophy, which FDR used to get us out of the Great Depression. But that is exactly what is not happening, not in the United States, not in Canada, Great Britain, Europe or Australia and certainly not in the Mideast. What is happening as a result of classic capitalism are social unrest and the implementation of war and police states worldwide.

Cameron says the whole problem is related to idleness of the workers and dependence on the State to take care of them. Krugman says the problem of idleness is the result of the waste of production resources that should be invested into the economy. For each the problem is simple: For Cameron it's the worker who doesn't work; for Krugman, the worker isn't given an opportunity to work. In austerity and a global trade philosophy (e. g. TPP) that pursues production to countries that provide the lowest wages and benefits, the result is a super rich class of billionaires and billions of people competing for lousy jobs.

But I believe in a third way to look at this, which is the ideology of slow growth, or degrowth, rather than never-ending growth and ravaging of resources. Paul Lafarge was Karl Marx's son-in-law. He wrote a testament called "The Right to Be Lazy", contending that a society that has developed so many resources surely can extend the right to idleness for everyone.

The essence of capitalism is eternal growth in a finite planet, which has resulted in a planet depleted of resources and a social surplus of people, about seven billion at this point, and climbing. Economist Paul Krugman feels capital should not sit idle but surge into circulation through the purchasing of goods and services. Unfortunately, the current socio-ecological crisis is telling us to end our profligate ways, slow growth, end our exploitation of resources and people and concentrate on social and ecological well-being. "Depense" is a word that refers to the expenditure of spending into the growth of spirituality and philosophy rather than private profits, to leave a forest alone, that to clear-cut the forest is actually counter-productive in the long run. Depense offers a process where we could collectively live "the good life". Pacifists Scott and Helen Nearing wrote a book called *The Good Life*, about the simplicity of working their farm in Vermont, relieving society from its illusory and meaningless pursuit of materialism.

The political leaders of the globe talk austerity while surrounded by opulence and greed. The social surplus that Marx talked about as the outcome of exploitation also results in the utilitarian wasting away of resources for profit.

We humans have always had all that we need for a basic standard of living without ruining the Earth in the process. Ancient societies consumed what they gathered and planted, but did not accumulate to excess. When economics entered the picture, it became a process of over-consumption for private profits and resulted in the mutilating of the planet. The powers that be expect us to cut back while the super rich accumulate more wealth. Their philosophy implies that not everyone can have a Ferrari. Classic economists call this zero-sum competition for personal growth, limits that allow consumption of resources for private profit. They lead us to believe that in a democracy everyone is able to pursue The American Dream, resulting in for example someone with a garage full of expensive vehicles (Bill Gates), an accumulation of material stuff beyond basic needs to give us "the good life."

A degrowth philosophy is one that tells us once basic needs are met (a nice house, a decent car, enough food, clothing, etc.), we have achieved the Good Life and don't need more. We need not clear a hillside of Douglas fir ("trees *are* the view", I saw recently on a bumper sticker), build up excessive expenditures, or vacations into space. All that we need is right here on Earth on our own tiny plot of land.

In significant numbers, there are growing movements in that direction. In small towns that have lost their jobs to free trade, and within urban sprawl that has no jobs, people are forming co-ops and a system of bartering to counter the capitalist philosophy. Indigenous land rights movements are playing pivotal roles worldwide, demanding an end to fossil fuel extraction, which ruins their land.

CHAPTER 3

One thing we must do is retake control of our legislatures. It is essential that we have public financing of elections. Right now corporations rule the legislatures by financing their campaign chests. Politicians have no choice but to follow the dictates of those who essentially hired them.

On any given day, more than 10,000 lobbyists swarm the nation's capitol paying off our "elected" officials. While our representatives in congress display never ending-campaign theatrics, behind the scenes lobbyists are impervious to election cycles, term limits, impeachment threats, restrictions, or regulations.

And after the elected officials terms are over, many of them proceed from there to some lucrative career with a major corporation, or become lobbyists themselves.

It's no secret to any of us that legislatures in Washington impose agendas that are not in the interests of the American people, but in the interests of major corporations. Here in my home state of Washington, Senators Patty Murray and Maria Cantwell and Governor Jay Inslee are all considered liberals—frustratingly liberal to the state's right wing base. And it is a fact that they are decent, hard-working politicians. On the other hand, they have no choice but to represent the interests of

Boeing, Microsoft, Amazon, and other major corporations in the state or their campaign money will dry up and they will be removed from office. Backdoor deals behind closed doors supersede the interests of the state's constituency. The result has been decreased corporate tax rates and regulations and increased spending on military expenditures for private defense contractors such as Boeing, one of the major corporations in the country that not only pays no corporate income tax, but actually get money back from the IRS.

Under Obama, Fannie Mae and Freddie Mac have been removed from government control and support, and there have been massive cuts in public programs.

These lobbyists prevent raises in the federal minimum wage, ease environmental regulations, and lobby in favor of tort reform aimed at limiting claims against pollution related illnesses and in favor of making it more difficult for debt-ridden citizens to file for bankruptcy.

The oil and gas industries have succeeded in removing themselves from regulations mandated by the Clean Air and Clean Water Acts, allowing fracking, offshore drilling, the blowing away of mountaintops, and other highly destructive practices.

They have succeeded in expanding the Bush-era tax cuts, which Obama signed into law.

What else we need to do, in fact have no choice but to do if we have any chance at all of survival is:

1. **Buy local.** Purchase goods and services with regional interest and keep money circulating locally and not abroad. Shopping at Walmart and Target allows most of the money to go to the corporate headquarters, with crumbs going to the workers. Investment in local energy represented in solar and wind, weatherization projects, mass transportation and investment in sustainable and regional projects such as methane energy from garbage rather than stinking landfills can work to reverse global warming and sustain the local economy. Shop at farmers' markets and local co-ops. Food should be grown for the domestic market, not in a monoculture/pesticide philosophy for export. It is healthier and better for the environment and society.

2. **Bank local.** Withdraw from major banks and put your money in local non-profit credit unions, which invest in the local economy rather than siphoning off our bank deposits to use for global speculation.

3. **Refuse, Reduce, Re-use and Recycle.** I know it all sounds pointless, and probably is, but we have to try. Avoid products that are designed on pur-

pose to wear out or go bad so we have to buy more. Re-use and repair clothes and restore the local cobbler rather than going to Nordstrom. Grow your own food as much as possible. Avoid meat that is not locally produced on small range free, grass-fed farms. Buy your lattes from local coffee shops and not Starbucks. Avoid bottled water. When someone gives you a plastic bottle at a party, ask if you can have tap water. It may not save us, but it will feed your soul. Ultimately, of course, refuse, reduce, re-use and recycle is impossible under capitalism, since the very essence of capitalism is to buy, consume or throw away, and buy more, as much and often as possible in a system of planned obsolescence. The earth cannot sustain such a philosophy, and thus it must cease.

4. **Create cooperatives.** Home health care workers, house cleaners, community kitchens, laundry workers, food co-ops, maintenance workers, and naturalists all are businesses that sustain the local economy.

5. **Have local control over resources.** Community-controlled forests will be more sustainably managed than the corporate model based on clear-cutting, with more local employment and profit, resulting in more concerns and interest in preserving the future environment. Increased local mass transit would provide more incentive for bicycling, busing and

walking. Walking or riding your bike to the local co-op and eating organically grown food will create a healthier society.

6. **Distribute the wealth.** Putting more people to work working fewer hours will create more job opportunities. A shorter workweek with equal distribution of wages increases opportunity for leisure, time with family, and creative interests. Produce and consume less. Americans are notorious for working too much and getting fewer vacations than the rest of the world (though that has changed with the local expansion of global economics).

7. **Create medical co-ops.** We need to create our own universal health care plan that is not run by the private health insurance industries and pharmaceuticals. Non-profits would be more interested in maintain the health of the people rather than profits for corporatists.

8. **Think before you buy.** Do you really need that Snickers bar (my favorite, darn it) or new pair of Nikes. If you have a sweet tooth, go to the local bakery (it will taste better anyway). If you need a new pair of shoes buy them locally, or at least American-made, if you can find it. Think about how much stuff you really need. Think sustainably rather than materially. And for God's sake, don't buy a Mercedes or

BMW. As you know from driving around, most of the people who have these vehicles are narcissistic road turkeys.

9. **Have nothing to do with Wall Street.** Wall Street does not build things or sustain society. It is simply a colossal gambling casino. Force businesses to profit from their manufacturing of goods, not speculation with our money. Revert our economy to one that provides for human needs, not private profits. End the billionaire class.

10. **Stop buying anything that has plastic in it.** Nobody said this was going to be easy, or even possible. But we have to try. We have no other choice at this point. If we stop buying plastic, they will stop making it.

11. **Quit voting Democrat.** I won't bother telling you to quit voting Republican, since it's doubtful any Republicans are reading this, or at least paying serious attention to it. Unless a Democrat is showing by his or her actions that he or she is committed to the above criteria, no Democrat is going to do the Earth or us any good.

12. **Become an artist.** We need to recognize art and its connection to community and spirit, not as a function of capitalism. Music, painting, writing, architecture; they're integral part of our spiritual

consciousness and our connection to Gaia. Record companies and Amazon are not.

13. **Build heavy and light rail.** Build more bicycle lanes. Create low-cost housing for the homeless and poor. Manage the land and stop development. Create only sustainable logging. Create shorter work-weeks and distribute the wealth equitably. Create a local currency.

It is also assumed that we cannot have high technology without relying on corporations such as Microsoft and Apple. Not true. In fact, local computer technicians could provide computer technology with more efficiency and with less impact on the environment because they would not operate on an obsession with private profits and planned obsolescence. Capitalism is based on the concept of consume and throw away as soon as possible so we have to buy more. It operates under the assumption that the earth has infinite resources, and that is its fatal flaw.

Our only chance is to end predator capitalism and corporate rule.

The recent movement of the sixties created a collective movement that is needed today without the selling out part that happened in the seventies. Demands for civil rights, an end to war, return to the land, and a spiritual renaissance that was represented in the writings of Thoreau and Scott and Helen Nearing challenged the status quo. Today we have the biggest challenge humankind has ever faced in nuclear proliferation and man-made global warming. We are going to have to force our leaders to act; they are not going to do it voluntarily. The most powerful adversary we have is the rich corporations who currently hold us and our elected leaders hostage. It's going to require the collective movement of all of us to break away from the predatory Capitalist paradigm.

Corporate bigwigs have drawn up the Trans Pacific Partnership (TPP) behind closed doors, and Congress has allowed Obama to

"fast track" the bill through without congressional oversight.

Leaked chapters of the TPP show that the environmental standards are even worse that previous trade agreements passed by Clinton, George W. Bush, and Obama. It is designed to increase fracking and offshore drilling in the U.S. for export to Europe and Asia. The agreement will give transnational corporations the legal right to sue governments if their environmental laws interfere with corporate profits—e.g., forcing Europe to start allowing GMO's.

Growing movements in the U.S. and around the world can stop this agreement and others like it. Movements around food safety, health, environmental and Internet freedom have been successful, and such movements can succeed against the TPP and the KXL pipeline. We can't depend on our leaders to end corporate greed. We must change our system of government so that it serves the people and the planet rather than the greed of corporate polluters and end the U.S. Empire military actions around the globe that safeguard corporate transnationals.

Obama will continue to lie to us that this agreement, and the Keystone XL pipeline will help the U.S. become more energy independent while providing jobs. But the truth is that these are designed to sell oil, methane gas, and coal on the international market and the jobs created will be minimal and short-lived.

Tar sands mining is one of the dirtiest, most polluting mining there is, and along with the increased use of trains to transport oil, coal, off-shore drilling, mountain top removal for coal, fracking for methane gas, and excavation for uranium for the development of more nuclear plants have all contributed to the environmental disaster that we inhabit. We have to act at the local level to stop it, since we can't rely on our so-called "elected" leaders.

The technology exists to transfer to carbon-free economy with alternate energy uses such as biofuel (locally produced only), solar, wind and tide—but that is contrary to the powerful oil, gas, and coal for-profit industries.

Understanding that imperialism and the global neoliberal economy are at odds with climate justice and a healthy planet must be our new imperative. Expanding wars around the globe are a part of that, as they keep the world safe for corporate greed and pollution.

Our society has been built around carbon and nuclear fuels and capitalism within a facade of democracy. A new economic system and new lifestyles are necessary to operate outside the current for-profit system. It is obvious that Barack Obama, Stephen Harper, and that elitist drug-criminal president in Mexico, Enrique Pena Nieto are all in cahoots with the transnationals, planet and people be damned. We must develop a global mindset that transcends their oppression.

This can be achieved at the local level through initiatives and incentives. In Seattle, we elected a socialist to the city council, passed a $15-an-hour minimum wage, developed local food resources, stopped coal trains from passing through the city, and have created local co-ops such as Puget Sound and Delridge Co-ops. We did this through local activism, not dependence on our leaders.

We need to wean ourselves off of plastics. We need to fix things rather than throwing them away and buying more to feed capitalist avarice. Millennials are abandoning cars (though unfortunately not smart phones) and instead walking, biking, using scooters and public transportation. We need to push for solar and geothermal energy through our municipalities rather than for-profit utility companies. We need to completely withdraw from Wall Street, a huge gambling casino that has done nothing productive outside of creating a billionaire class. We need to build a local economy that produces and consumes here rather than transported from China or Vietnam. Strong community action sends chills through the spines of corporations and politicians. We need to let them know that we will no longer tolerate their for-profit philosophy that has brought the planet to the brink of ruin.

And most importantly, global neoliberal trade agreements that undermine sovereignty and democracy must be rescinded and stopped.

CONCLUSION

As we observe the melting of the ice caps and the daily horror stories about catastrophic storms, devastating droughts, flooding away of homes, regional conflicts, mass migrations and starvation, I am dazed and confused by the ostensibly apathetic response of our government, the media, and much of the population, though the latter is starting to come out of its sleepwalk.

Recently I was talking to a young hippie-ish like woman with her three kids in tow about my book about the boomers: *What Happened to the Love Generation? How the Boomers Blew It.* I was speaking in general terms about the state of the environment, and she cut me off by saying: "I like to be more positive thinking." I responded knee jerk style: "Good luck with that." I understand: She's young and she has three young children. Unfortunately, putting our heads in the sand isn't going to fix the situation. This mass form of denial is actually scary. It means that by not facing facts nothing is going to be done to fix the problem. It's like ignoring obvious symptoms of cancer and not going to the doctor for treatment until it is too late.

In the 70's, when the working class in the United States, Europe, Japan, Australia and New Zealand were attaining middle-class lifestyles (the so-called "second world" Baltic states and the "third world" of Latin America, Asia, and Africa were somehow left out of this equation), due to New Deal actions in the U.S. and the Marshall Plan in Europe, the U.S. Federal Reserve began printing "fiat" money, oftentimes described as "toilet paper money" because it was no longer backed by gold or silver. Along with that occurred a beginning transfer of the manufacturing base to the Third World that did not have a well-paid working class but instead a slave-wage class. This led to a financial asset movement with financial securities and a massive rise of a financial elite with monstrous economic power and unprecedented political influence. Financial regulations and market controls were eliminated, which led to the acceleration of global speculation. This was prodded along most markedly in the Reagan administration in the U.S. and Margaret Thatcher in Great Britain.

The digital revolution that followed spurred global speculation even more, using a "free-market" philosophy as justification for the creation of a new billionaire class. Households began having to have both partners working in order to maintain the middle-class lifestyles they had become accustomed to, and when that didn't work they began to use credit cards that were being issued to them like candy. A debt economy was created, in which debt was just moved around and maintained indefinitely.

Households began to borrow more money, using the value of their homes as collateral. The global marketplace was also using credit, which resulted in financial instability globally. Capitalist investors speculated recklessly rather than providing real goods and services.

This led directly to the financial crash of 2008, and the "too big to fail banks" philosophy that mandated rescuing them to avoid global economic collapse.

With new money in their hands, they just carried on as before, knowing that the government will be there to rescue them, which has led to another financial bubble until where today in 2015, it is estimated that there is $70 trillion in global "shadow" banks. Consumer debt continued to pile up, which spread to local municipalities now also in debt, unable to maintain infrastructure and conspiring to end the pension trusts that they had "guaranteed" to local government workers. Property and other taxes were added to the already overburdened working class. An underclass of homeless increased by millions. Speculative investments such as hedge funds replaced real investments such as into manufacturing and services.

Established economists, most of whom studied classic capitalist economics in college, even Nobel Prize winners such as Paul Krugman and Joseph Stieglitz, are thus stuck in this paradigm of capitalist thought, their study of Marxism marginal at best. Even some Marxist scholars, and certainly Marxist critics, are hung up on Volume I of *Capital* in which Marx discusses production and its relation to surplus value, which is put into the hands of the employer to exploit the worker. Marx died before he could finish Volume III, leaving a tangle of notes for Engels to try to delineate. Marx meant to elaborate on banking and credit—which is essential to understanding what is happening today.

The U.S. worker is still trying to recover from the 2008 collapse. What little manufacturing base that has returned has been in slave-wage jobs with few benefits. The U.S. workers have returned to their credit cards to maintain the economy. In Europe, it's even worse, as a neoliberal mandate of austerity has been instituted by the "troika" the IMF, the European Commission, and the European Central Bank—and agreed to by a solvent Germany; and in countries such as Spain, Ireland, Italy, France, and especially Greece, they are finding less work available while having their previously guaranteed pensions and other benefits reduced or eliminated. The people of Greece have pretty much had enough and elected a socialist government, but it too has bowed to the merciless demands of Merkel, and Germany.

There is a constant circle of governments giving bankers money. The banks speculate recklessly, go under, and go back to the government for more bailouts. Along with this is a massive credit economy created by consumers who can't afford it, but have no choice but to use their credit cards to maintain their marginal lifestyles, pay the rent or mortgage, send their kids to school, and put food on the table. The lower classes rely on fast food, which is cheaper than the food in the supermarket. An underclass of homeless balloons. Credit and slow economic growth also increases government debt—and thus a constant federal deficit. The U.S. owes China an absurd amount of dollars, apparently many trillions. Household debt has increased due to capitalist policies of global free trade, union destruction, and mass layoffs. This means less production of goods and services, leading to businesses unable to generate income. Small farms, factories, and restaurants go under. Local governments default on their loans and can no longer support pensions, infrastructure or schools. Prison populations increase, and are privatized. All these changes contribute to a chain reaction, from increased debt to asset price collapse. The financial asset prices are boosted artificially during housing and debt phases, which leads to another financial bubble—which we are in now. More debt is accumulated to avoid default.

Classic capitalist economic principles hypothesized that prices always adjusted to supply and demand. When this didn't work,

Keynesian economics was implemented, such as FDR's New Deal, creating a two-price system—which delayed Marx's prediction of concentration of wealth at the top. Keynesian economics was attacked and abandoned during Reagan, and a credit economy was created, using fiat money printed by the Fed and distributed to the banks. While investment increased, wages and income didn't. The U.S. Bank and Federal Reserve loaned trillions of dollars out to the banks. But not a cent was given to the millions of homeowners who had their houses repossessed. Minimal regulations such as the Dodd-Frank Act were implemented, which did little or nothing, and business carried on as usual, with more reckless global speculation in globally, mostly in hedge funds, further delaying total economic collapse.

Our world economy is essentially a giant Ponzi scam, exploiting our world's resources and people to put more and more money into the hands of the super rich.

International law prohibits military attacks on other nations unless those actions are in defense of "imminent danger" to the home state. ISIS is interested in toppling the existing corrupt and U.S. sponsored political regimes in the Muslim world and not in attacking the U.S. itself. Obama has said

as much: "…we have not yet determined specific plotting against our homeland…"

In order to legitimize his criminal air war, Obama introduced the world to a new "terror cell" no one had ever heard of called "the Khorsan group" in order to appear consistent with international law.

We need to ask ourselves the real reasons the U.S. is launching a war against ISIS while also supporting Israel's murderous campaign against the Palestinians, which last summer resulted in the killing of over 500 children.

In the 1990s under Clinton, over half a million children in Iraq died from U.S.-imposed sanctions. U.S. Secretary of State Madeline Albright responded to a question from CBS's Leslie Stahl in regard to this atrocity: "We think the price is worth it." A military source told journalist Jeremy Scahill about the standard Special Forces operation in the age of Obama: "If there's one person they're going after and there are 34 other people in the building, then 35 people are going to die."

Thus we have a wedding party where women, children and elderly are slaughtered and the person they are after gets away.

In Afghanistan and Iraq, innocent people have been killed routinely in two unending wars that have been dubious at best from the start.

The difference between ISIS's beheading a few journalists and the atrocities committed from Bush 1 through the

Obama administration is a matter of scale. The number of deaths in Iraq caused by U.S.

sanctions and attacks are over three million, and counting, including 750 children, according to Amnesty International.

Add to this the tortures committed in Abu Grahib, Guantanamo and elsewhere with the endorsement of the Chief Executive.

The U.S. and Israel kill Muslims and Arabs routinely, treating the innocents killed as "collateral damage."

On the campaign trail in 2007, Obama said over and over: "…it's time to stop spending billions of dollars trying to put Iraq back together and start spending the money putting America back together."

We're still waiting.

The escalation of military action in Iraq and Syria is fueling Middle Eastern jihadism. ISIS videos of beheadings only infuses their movement with greater publicity and power, because they know it prompts action by the Obama administration and thus makes them hate Americans even more. It comes straight out of the playbook of Osama bin Laden.

Our longtime alliance with Middle Eastern despots and with Arab princes and sultans further feeds jihadist sentiments, along with our backing of Israel. The jihadists are far from advancing popular democracy, but they also know that American democracy is a farce. Al Qaeda, and now ISIS, have convinced their supporters—right or wrong—that Islam is under attack by America. They believe that their lands, their communities, and their religion is being threatened by the most powerful military in the world. The longer we are in the region, the more their movement grows. As Obama once said himself: "There is no military solution in Iraq."

Of course, there is only one reason why we colonize the area militarily, and that is because of oil. Our domestic problems of plutocracy, inequality, poverty and ecocide of minorities in our towns and cities are only exasperated by global colonialism. The U.S. campaigns abroad to further concentrate wealth and power and to continue burning vast quantities of fossil fuels for trillions of dollars of private profit, feeding nationalism at home and stealing resources from other states, has brought the world to the brink of economic and ecological disaster. While the media obsesses about Islamic beheadings, civilization is heading for a disaster of epic proportions, all because we won't end our obsession with a destructive economic principle: for-profit capitalism.

President Obama was elected on bold promises to the American people and elected again as the obvious lesser of two evils, and because it was obvious to the corporations that he was going to continue with a pro-corporate/pro capitalist agenda. The financial crisis of 2008 could have been an opportunity for him to become an FDR like hero or then assassinated and become a martyr, and to precipitate revolution. Instead, it has been business as usual, with carbon emissions reaching unprecedented levels, social unrest here at home and globally, a fascist militarization of the police, and huge income disparity.

Of course, what held Obama back beside cowardice and narcissism was that he isn't in charge. He's as much a puppet on strings as was Reagan, Clinton, and the Bushes, or for that matter, Carter. An ideology based on private profits is in charge. And that simply is what must change.

The Back to the Land movement that frittered away in the 70s could have created co-op communities that used organic farming which experts have shown actually create higher yields, not to mention less pollution, global warming, and disease from pesticide use. It could have stopped the major corporate agri-businesses from managing our food intake. Instead, we have powerful "philanthropists" such as Bill Gates infecting small farms in India and Asia with GMOs that destroy the land and drive small farmers to starvation and suicide.

There is a profound gap between the capitalists and the ecologists in their perception of the world, and many ecologists don't see it. Capitalists see economic growth as linear and infinite, while ecologists see nature as cyclical. Unfortunately, many ecologists buy into the capitalist philosophy that rules, because after all, they are part of a capitalist system too.

When the ice melts in the Arctic, capitalists see opportunities, such as drilling for oil or more accessible shipping routes. Ecologists see this as an alarming consequence of global warming. Capitalists put their heads in the sand about global warming, because all they can see is short-term profits. Capitalists don't concern themselves with more destructive storms, melting ice caps, and a rising sea level that is already washing away expensive homes on sea shores around the world. Not only couldn't they care less, they look for opportunities. What they are simply incapable of seeing, or else care about is that growth on a finite planet is unsustainable. They have literally used up the support systems for sustainability. Despite the fact that we are able to (or forced to) live in an ever more complicated high-tech world civilization, we are still dependent on the Earth's normal systems that ultimately sustain us.

To put this in nutshell perspective, historical civilizations used fishing as a means of subsistence, to feed oneself and one's family. When fishing became an economic tool, as a means for monetary profit, overfishing resulted. People in the cities grow fat from restaurant fish, but the poor fisherman in Somalia (for example) has no more fish in the sea to feed his family and is forced to become a pirate, which like all forms of criminality (gangster mobs, drugs, etc.), is just another function of capitalism.

And today, the demand for an ever-expanding economy has surpassed the sustainability yield of the ecosystem. The result has been loss of topsoil, overuse of pesticides and herbicides and GMOs to keep capitalism running, the overgrazing on rangeland and the deterioration of the desert. These are the results of an economic system based on private profits. We are witnessing this ecological deficit in places such as California and Australia, with droughts threatening convenient lifestyles of watering lawns and golf courses. Even here where I live in the State of Washington, which is famous for its rain, the governor has declared a state emergency because of "drought", not due to lack of rain, but lack of snow in the mountains, which we depend on for our water.

As national disasters increase, so do our insurance rates, since insurances companies, after all, are also in the business of profit. This too has obvious economic consequences, when the insurance rates become too excessive to pay. More and more, the federal government is called on for cleanup of these disasters, increasing a federal deficit that also is unsustainable.

Democracy today has been overwhelmed by a sophisticated group of elites that enforce their own rules, promoting materialism and domination over nature. They imprison, infiltrate, kill, torture, and do whatever they can get away with regardless of morality or laws. Look at Chelsea

Manning, Julian Assange, and Edward Snowden. Snowden and Assange don't dare return to the United States to stand trial since they are quite aware of the consequences of exposure of government malfeasance if they do.

We can't even rely on our electoral system, since a plutocracy holds power that thwarts democracy. Those politicians and activists who had a powerful effect on the populace were shut down. The sixties was the last time the establishment felt threatened by a progressive movement—until today. In the sixties they resorted to assassinations: the Kennedy's, MLK, Malcolm X, Medger Evers, Fred Hampton—all assassinated. Obama is only doing what he is told to do: Deceive us with eloquence, and then carry on with the capitalist program.

It is not wrong to break the law when that law is destroying the Earth. In fact, to do so is a moral responsibility, as Martin Luther King, Jr. so eloquently said. And since species are going extinct at an unprecedented rate, a radical response is urgently needed, since the political system has not done its part to rescue the environment.

Look at what is happening in poor communities today. The police are being filmed killing people for the least amount of resistance: running, protesting loudly, or not doing anything at all, such as answering a doorbell. And the people are reacting and getting positive response. President Obama has even said that no more military equipment will be issued to municipalities.

Since the agri-capitalist-industrial system is fundamentally destructive and inherently unsustainable, and since the current situation is so dire, direct action has become obligatory.

Direct action when convenient (not putting oneself in a vulnerable situation, such as being arrested and going to prison) must work together with passive resistance. Earth First! and the Sierra Club need to recognize that they have common goals and should be working together, just as the Democrats and Republicans work together to please the corporations while pretending to be at opposite ends. Civil disobedience combined with active resistance (such as actions by Greenpeace and the Sea Shepherd) can be segue into transforming public opinion and power, changing behavior, laws, and policies.

Authorities have been successful using tactics that are violent and framed to justify to the public that their spying, infiltration, police and military violence are necessary responses for the public good. Drone strikes are an example of this deceit, since the reality is that they are only making the Muslims community angrier and more radical.

Historically, such repression has succeeded in eviscerating the resistance. The Movement in the sixties is a palpable example. But today, these actions are being filmed, and more difficult for the elitists to rationalize.

Antics of Earth First! and the Earth Liberation Front have had modest successes we must look to as we examine what we can do. In 1996 thousands of citizens in California turned out to protest the logging of old-growth timber by the Pacific Lumber Co. More than a

1,000 people were arrested. But this resistance led to a law that has protected at least some of the precious old-growth groves that are thousands of years old.

Major protests and resistance led to the U.S. Forest Service under President Clinton to issue the Roadless Conservation Rule, which has protected some 60 million acres of federal forestland.

Direct action as resistance is slowly having a positive effect. Protests against the KXL pipeline have resulted in the Obama administration's inclined against allowing it to be built, at least until the next administration takes over.

There were massive protests here in Seattle because Shell posted a 300-foot high drilling machine in Elliott Bay while it was being repaired before shipping up to the Chukchi Sea to drill off the Alaskan North Slope, one of the most dangerous spots in the world due to severe storms. A spill similar to the Horizon disaster in the Gulf of Mexico would be disastrous for sea animals, including whales and walruses. There are growing campaigns worldwide to ban offshore drilling, but President Obama has allowed it anyway in his usual manner of saying one thing and doing another.

A groundswell of citizen action is emerging, not just locally and nationally, but globally.

Seattle has banned coal trains from passing through the city. The majority of people polled throughout the world are opposed to coal trains and export terminals, fracking, tar sands removal, in addition to offshore drilling—but the predatory corporations are determined to proceed despite it all, and currently they have the legal right to proceed because of obsequious politicians.

The Lummi have protested the coal export terminal in Bellingham, Washington. The Lower Elwha Klallam tribe in Washington State succeeded in having two dams removed in the Elwha River because they were killing salmon runs. The indigenous populations in the Northwest are cognizant more than anyone of how the salmon runs have been decimated.

Heartfelt politicians such as Bernie Sanders and Elizabeth Warren are putting fear into the core political framework in Washington D.C. And the people are responding favorably to these two because they are aware that the current system doesn't work for the people. Sanders even calls himself a socialist, albeit a "democratic" socialist.

Instead of subsidizing drilling and pipelines for short-term jobs, profit for the corporations and permanent damage to the environment, the government should be subsidizing solar, wind public transit, high-speed rail, retrofits and renewable energy.

And this all must begin at the local level, as Seattle is doing, to bolster local economies and strengthen the public sphere. People have come to realize through socialists such as City Council person Kshama Sawant that housing homeless, for example, is actually cheaper than doing nothing, not to mention contributing to a safer, more compassionate society.

On the global level, we must end the parasitic World Trade imperialist model and allow indigenous people to return to that which has always sustained them. We must abandon the parasitic fossil-fueled, throwaway economy that has brought us to the brink. We need to abandon nuclear energy and begin the arduous process of cleanup. We need a society for the commons built on solar/hydrogen/ wind, and an urban transport system built on modern day rail. We need a comprehensive consciousness and undertaking to refuse/reduce/reuse/recycle. And probably most importantly, we need to reduce the population. None of this can be accomplished under a capitalist economy.

In our capitalist culture we are led to believe that the rich are deserving of their wealth because they are smarter, work harder, and are more creative than the rest of us. And an obedient media perpetuates this myth by presenting Bill Gates and others of his ilk as heroes because of not only this but because of their philanthropic activities. We are led to believe that capitalism is a charitable institution in of itself because the wealth filters down on the rest of us who are willing to work hard. Capitalism mechanisms are called superior to any other system because it creates economic and social progress, and free-market capitalism is the solution to all the problems of the world.

In fact, the exact opposite is true. Capitalism maintains its wealth for the very rich, casts crumbs to the workers, and causes all the world's problems. Poverty, resource depletion, species extinction, pollution, overpopulation, perpetual war and global warming are all a direct result of capitalism.

And charitable activities actually perpetuate inequality by deflecting the fact that the top 1% maintains the wealth and power of the world and that 84 individuals have more wealth than 50% of the world's population.

It also presents the fantasy that government efforts to ease social ills is wasteful and ineffective while business, with its obsession on the bottom line and by applying market principles to the social body is the only answer. In this mindset, we are even trending toward police and military privatization—along with schools and prisons.

This myth is preserved with the Bill and Melinda Gates Foundation and grandiose gestures by monomaniacs such as Bono and Angelina Jolie, which lead us to believe that they are curing the world's social ills. The fact is, these actions may help a little temporarily, but solve nothing. Theoretically, if philanthropy worked we wouldn't have any problems, would we? But in fact the problems only get worse. Bill Gates investment with Monsanto's GMO's in Africa are only wrecking the land, ruining people's health and creating more poverty. Sean Penn's work in Haiti solved nothing; poverty there is worse than ever.

The ultimate answer to all this is of course to abandon capitalism, and adopt an egalitarian socialist society. It's probably too late, but we have to at the very least try. And we must do it with a consciousness of spirituality, creativity and empathy. Then perhaps we can obtain a positive sense of joy working together in much smaller agrarian communities absent of the insatiable greed of global capitalism.

October 2015

BIBLIOGRAPHY

PART I: FREE MARKET CAPITALISM

Anthony Andrady, *Plastics and the Environment*, CABI Publishing

Christopher Anderson, *What Happened to the Love Generation? How the Boomers Blew It*, Outskirts Press

Joel Balken, *The Corporation: The Pathological Pursuit of Profit and Power*, The New York Press

Jack Barnes, *Capitalism's World Disorder*, Pathfinder Press

Lester R. Brown, *Eco-economy*, Earth Policy Institute

Norman Birnbaun, *The Radical Renewal*, Pantheon Books

Norm Chomsky, *Failed States: The Abuse of Power and the Assault on Democracy*, Metropolitan Books

Charles Darwin, *The Origin of Species* The Guardian, *General Augusto Pinochet* and *Muammar al-Gaddafi*

Todd Gitlen, *The Sixties: Years of Hope and Rage*, Bantam Books

Naomi Klein, *The Shock Doctrine*

James Lovelock, *The Ages of Gaia: A Biography of Our Living Earth*, W. W. Norton Library of Economics and Liberty, *Milton Friedman*

Herbert Marcuse, *One Dimensional Man: Studies in the Ideology of Advanced Industrial Society*

Dwight Macdonald, *Against the American Grain*, Random House National Archives and Records Administration, *The Marshall Plan*

John Perkins, *Confessions of an Economic Hit Man*, Ebury Press New Republic, *Hyak, Friedman, and the Illusions of Conservative Economics*

Ayn Rand, *The Fountainhead* and *Atlas Shrugged*

Jean Edward Smith, *FDR*, Random House

The Supreme Court Industrial Society, *John Marshall* USHistory.org, *Thomas Jefferson*

PART TWO: MARX AND MARXISM

Jake Barnes, *Capitalism's World Disorder*, Pathfinder Press

Isaiah Berlin, *Karl Marx: His Life and Environment.* Oxford University Press

Norman Birnbaun, *The Radical Renewal: The Politics of Ideas in Modern America*, Pantheon Books

James Brophy, *Popular Culture and the Public Sphere in the Rhineland.* Cambridge University Press

John W. Burrow *The Crisis of Reason: European Thought 1848-1914*, Yale University Press

Geoff Eley, *Forging Democracy: The History of the Left in Europe, 1850-2000*, Oxford University Press

Michael Harrington, *Socialism Past & Future*, Little, Brown & Co

Alfred Kelly, *The Descent of Darwin: The Popularization of Darwin in German 1860-1914*, University of North Carolina Press

Karl Marx, *The Communist Manifesto.*

Eric Pooley, *The Climate War*-Hyperion, 2010

David McClellan, *Karl Marx, a Biography*, Palgrave MacMillan

John Stuart Mill, *Principles of Political Economy*, D. Appleton and Co

Bernard H. Moss, *The Socialism of Skilled Workers*, University of Berkeley Press

Eric Roll, *A History of Economic Thought*, Faber and Faber

Paul Laurence Rose, *Revolutionary Anti-Semitism in Germany From Kant to Wagner*, Princeton University Press

Paul Thomas, *Karl Marx and the Anarchists*. Routledge Press

Francis Wheen, *Karl Marx, a Life*, W. W. Norton & Co.

Timothy Miller, *Tolstoy Farm, Roots of Communal Revival, 1962-1966*

PART THREE: DARWIN AND EXTINCTION

John Alroy, *A Multispecies Overkill Simulation of the End-Pleistocene Megafaunal Mass Extinction*, Science

Michael Benton, *When Life Nearly Died: The Greatest Mass Extinction of All Time*, Thames and Hudson

Tim Birkheas, *How Collectors Killed the Great Auk*, New Scientist

James Bowen and Margarita Brown, *The Great Barrier Reef: History, Science and Heritage*, Cambridge University Press

James H. Brown, *Macroecology*, University of Chicago Press

Alan Burdick, *Out of Eden: An Odyssey of Ecological Invasion*, Farrar, Straus and Giroux

Rachel Carson, *Silent Spring*, Houghton Mifflin

Claudine Cohen, *The Fate of the Mammoth: Fossils, Myth, and History*, University of Chicago Press

Paul J. Crutzen, "Geology of Mankind" Nature Magazine

Charles Darwin, *The Origin of Species*, Harvard University Press

Mark Davis, *Invasion Biology*, Oxford University Press

Jared Diamond, *Guns, Germs and Steel: The Fates of Human Societies*, Norton

A. Hallam and P.B. Wignal, Mass Extinctions and Their Aftermaths, Oxford University Press

Stephen Hawking, A Brief History of Time, Bantam Books Trade Paperbacks

Richard E. Leakey and Roger Levin, The Sixth Extinction: Patterns of Life and the Future of Humankind, Anchor Press

Barry Lopez, Arctic Dreams and Of Wolves and Men, Vintage Press

Bill McKibben, The End of Nature, Random House

Jonathon Schell, The Fate of the Earth, Knopf

Josh Fox, Gasland, a film

PART FOUR: WHAT WE CAN DO

Lester R. Brown, Eco-Economy, Earth Policy Institute

Amy Goodman, The Exception to the Rulers: Exploring Oily Politicians, War Profiteers and the Media that Love them, Hyperion James Hansen blog

Scott and Helen Nearing, The Good Life

Raj Patel, The Value of Nothin, How to Reshape Market Society and Redefine Democracy

Alan Thein Durning, This Place on Earth, Sasquatch Books

Alan Weisman, The World Around Us, St. Martin's Press

Naomi Wolf, The End of America, Chelsea Green Publishing

Howard Zinn, Terrorism and War, Seven Stories and Original Zinn, Harper's